Contents

unit 1 **Word classes**

VERB?...
ADVERB?..

Key idea

Words are categorised in classes according to the jobs they do in a sentence. Words can belong to more than one class.

Noun
Name of thing or feeling:
common nouns: e.g. *flower, computer, ships*
proper nouns: e.g. *Carolyn, Scotland, August*
collective nouns: e.g. *team, herd, gang*
abstract nouns: e.g. *beauty, honesty, wisdom*

Pronoun:
Stands in place of preceding noun:
personal: e.g. *I, you, it, she, we, they*
possessive: e.g. *mine, his, theirs*
reflexive: e.g. *myself, herself, themselves*
relative: e.g. *who, which, that*

Verb
Shows action or state of being:
past: I *kicked* the ball.
present: I *kick* the ball.
future: I *will kick* the ball.

Adverb
Describes or modifies a verb, an adjective or another adverb:
verb + adverb: He walked *quickly*.
adverb + adjective: She felt *slightly* nervous.
adverb + adverb: They played *very* skilfully.

Adjective
Describes or modifies a noun or a pronoun:
e.g. *the bouncing baby* boy

Preposition
Shows the relationship between words or groups of words:
e.g. *at, in, to, by, with*

Interjection
An exclamation:
e.g. *Oh!* and *Ow!*

Conjunction (connective)
Links ideas in clauses and sentences:
e.g. *Consequently*, he was too hot *and* too tired to play.

ALERT
Words like *a, an, the, this, that, each* and *several* are types of adjectives called "determiners".

(20 marks)

In the sentences below, say to which class each word in bold type belongs.

1   In some countries, many people get their water from a **well**.

2   My brother was ill last week, but now he is quite **well**.

3   Your sister sang really **well** at the concert last night.

4   Whenever Mrs Wilson thinks of her dead husband, tears **well** up in her eyes.

5   Jack fell **down**.

6   Jill fell **down** the hill too.

7   The quilt was stuffed with duck **down**.

8   **Pass** the salt, please.

9   You cannot enter some buildings unless you have a **pass**.

10 King Solomon was known for his **wisdom**.

The following sentences refer to sentences 1–10 above. Are they true or false? If you think a sentence is false, change it so that it is true.

11 In (1), **countries, people** and **water** are nouns.

12 In (2), **was** and **is** are verbs.

13 There is a possessive adjective in both (2) and (3).

14 In (4), the word **thinks** is a plural noun.

15 There is a proper noun in both (5) and (6).

16 In (6), the word **too** is an adverb.

17 There are two prepositions in (7).

18 In (8) **please** is a verb.

19 In (9), **unless** is a conjunction that links two clauses.

20 There are two prepositions in (10).

(20 marks – 0.5 mark for each correct answer)

In the sentences below, say to which class each word in bold type belongs. Is it a noun, pronoun, adjective or adverb?

1. Mr Jordan blamed **himself** for the **mistake**.
2. We don't need those old boxes, so **you** can throw **them** away.
3. Be **careful**, Sue. That knife is **very** sharp.
4. **Who** taught you to paint so **skilfully**?
5. Is there **anything** else you need for the party **tomorrow**?
6. Turn **left** when you pass the **next** corner.
7. I found the key, **which** was in the **box**.
8. **Too many** people are in the lift.
9. **Honesty** is the **best** policy.
10. **He** was eating like there was no **tomorrow**.

Choose the right word from the brackets.

11. Is this bolt (difference, different) from the other ones?
12. Are you going to come with Peter and (I, me) or stay here?
13. We've managed to repair your bike (successful, successfully), so you can use it now.
14. Sometimes it is not (easy, easily) for a fox to escape from (it's, its) hunters.
15. A police officer stopped our car and asked to see Dad's driving (licence, license).
16. When we go home, I'll ask my (Mother, mother) if you can come and stay with us for a few (days', days) next month.
17. Jack is a very (skilful, skillful) driver, so he has never had (no, an) accident.
18. The (advice, advise) from his doctor was to exercise (regular, regularly).
19. She (passed, past) her exam just this (passed, past) week.
20. I think that (were, was) a (flock, herd) of cattle in the distant field.
21. (There's, Theirs, Their's) is the house with the (bad, badly) painted front door.
22. We managed to cook the dinner (ourself, ourselves), (but, because, when) it would not have won any prizes!

Oh!

(20 marks – 0.5 mark for each correct answer)

In the sentences below, say to which class each word in bold type belongs.

1. We **live** not far **from** the centre of a small town.

2. **Oh!** Don't creep up on **me** like that. You made me jump!

3. Last week the river burst its banks and **flooded** several fields **but** the water did not reach our house.

4. We like to watch "**Who** wants to be a millionaire?" **on** television.

5. February is **usually** a **cold** month and this year was no exception.

Write two different words that can be used in each space below. Use the type of word shown in brackets.

6. I _____(verb) your shoes are _____(preposition) the cupboard, _____(proper noun).

7. _____ (pronoun) left this bag _____ (preposition) a tree in the park.

8. _____(exclamation)! How _____ (adjective) to see you again after such a long time!

9. Motorists who drive _____ (adverb) and cause _____ (noun) may be sent to prison.

10. Mike is tall _____ (conjunction) he is not a fast runner.

11. _____ (noun) make very _____ (adjective) pets.

12. A large number of baby kangaroos might be called a _____ (collective noun) of joeys!

13. _____ (adverb) I realised that I was _____ (verb) in a haunted house.

Extra challenge

Make up three different sentences of your own based on the following sentence structure:

The [adjective] [noun] [adverb] [verb] the [adjective] [noun] [preposition] the [noun].

Here's an example: *The demented dog crazily chased the frightened cat around the garden.*

unit 2

Using standard English

Key idea

We can use non-standard English in speech, but we must use standard English in formal written work.

- Verbs must agree with their subject.
- Pronouns must agree with the words to which they refer or which they replace.
- We have to be consistent in the use of tenses.
- We cannot use double negatives such as "I haven't done nothing".
- In formal work, we do not use non-standard (slang, colloquial or dialect) expressions.

Try it out!

Choose the right word from the brackets. *(14 marks)*

1 Where (is, are) the rest of our luggage?

2 (Has, Have) you brought the box of chocolates with you?

3 There (is, are) more than one cause for most of the crimes committed in big cities.

4 Jonathan (has, have) broken the school long-jump record.

5 Everything (is, are) ready for the party, isn't it?

6 Everybody (has, have) replied to the invitations, haven't they?

7 Neither the referee nor the players (was, were) involved in the fight on the pitch.

8 Fifty kilometres (is, are) a long way to walk in a single day.

9 Half of that food (is, are) unfit to eat.

10 Half of these bananas (is, are) unripe and that apple (is, are) rotten.

11 The high cost of new houses and flats (has, have) a bad effect on many families.

12 This pair of scissors (is, are) quite sharp, but those scissors (is, are) blunt.

Keep practising!

Choose the right words from the brackets. *(8 marks)*

1. Dr Newman always locks her car when (he, she) parks it at the Health Centre.

2. Paul told us, "I blame (meself, myself) for the mistake. I was in too much of a hurry to finish the job."

3. I haven't seen (anybody, nobody) leaving or entering our neighbour's house for several days.

4. (Maybe, May be) they are all on holiday overseas.

5. You could be right. We haven't seen (nothing, anything) of them for at least a fortnight.

6. Sometimes my dad has to work at night. Then he starts work at about 11 p.m. and (come, comes, came) home at about 730 the following morning.

7. He usually goes to bed after lunch and then gets up when I (am, was) just going to bed.

8. Your old bike is no good now. There isn't (nothing, anything) we can do to make it safe to ride again, so you may as well get rid of it.

Take up the challenge!

What more formal expressions can we use instead of the underlined words?
(8 marks)

1. Be careful! Mum will <u>blow her top</u> if she hears you speak like that.

2. Our new car is really <u>out of this world</u>.

3. Every child seems to think that a mobile phone is <u>a must</u> now.

4. The new sports centre has proved to be <u>a big hit</u> in our district.

5. After the game, Mary felt <u>dead beat</u> and had to sit down and rest.

6. After a while, I get <u>fed up</u> watching television and prefer to play a game or chat with my friends.

7. Granddad says that school is not as tough for <u>kids</u> as it was when he was young.

8. When my parents started their own security business, they really <u>hit the jackpot</u>.

7

Active and passive verbs 1

🔑 Key idea

Verbs can be in the active or passive voice.

- When we use an active verb, the action goes from the subject to the object:

    My friend kicked the ball very hard.

- When we use a passive verb, the action goes from the verb back to the subject:

    The goalkeeper was knocked out by a boot.

We often use a passive verb when:
- We do not know who did an action, e.g. *My bike was stolen during the night.*
- We are more interested in what happened to somebody than in the person or thing that did it.

Try it out!

When there is a serious traffic accident, the following things might happen. Put in the passive form of the verbs. Use *is* or *are*, as in these examples:

*Sometimes a car **is hit** by a lorry. Then people **are injured** or **killed**.*
(10 marks)

1   Sometimes the road _____ (block).

2   The police _____ (notify) by somebody using a mobile phone.

3   An ambulance _____ (send) to the scene of the accident.

4   People _____ (trap) inside a car and cannot get out.

5   Injured people _____ (rescue) and _____ (take) to hospital in an ambulance.

6   Signs _____ (put) up to warn other road-users.

7   Traffic _____ (divert) if possible.

8   Witnesses _____ (question) by the traffic police to find out what happened.

9   Damaged vehicles _____ (tow) away so that traffic can use the road again.

10 The relatives of any dead or injured people _____ (inform) by the police.

Keep practising!

Put in the *passive Simple Past* form of the verbs in brackets. *(10 marks)*

One of the world's biggest earthquakes occurred off the north-western tip of Sumatra. Two gigantic "plates" collided below the seabed. One plate (1)_____ (force) up along a line many kilometres long. When the land rose, a huge quantity of water (2)_____ (push) upwards and outwards. As a result, big tsunami waves (3)_____ (create).

Coastal regions of Sumatra, Thailand, Sri Lanka and India (4) _____ (batter) by the waves. People (5)_____ (sweep) away, homes (6)_____ (destroy) and hundreds of thousands of people (7)_____ (kill). Many unlucky people (8)_____ (bury) under the debris caused by the waves. In some cases, their bodies (9)_____ (find) by rescuers but, in many cases, no traces remained of the missing people. Throughout the world, concerts and other special events (10)_____ (hold) to raise money for the victims.

Take up the challenge!

Rewrite these sentences. If the sentence is in the active voice, change it to passive. If it is passive, change it to active. *(10 marks)*

1   Lightning struck the barn.
2   The referee was hit by the flying ball.
3   I sent the letter by email.
4   We washed and polished the car on Saturday.
5   Meat is not eaten by vegetarians.
6   We were drenched by the rain.
7   The slow tortoise won the race.
8   The magician kept us amazed for hours.
9   Our teacher is liked by everyone in our class.
10 I cooked the dinner, so my brother washed the dishes.

unit 4

Connectives

Key idea

Connectives are words and phrases that are used to link different parts of a text. They can join words, phrases, clauses, sentences and paragraphs. Connecting words and phrases do different jobs:

Addition	Time	Cause and effect	Opposition
Adds additional information	Shows when things happen	Shows that one thing is the result of another	Shows a contrast or a different point of view
and	next	because	although
also	soon	so	however
or	afterwards	since	but
besides	until	as	yet
furthermore	when	if	despite
in addition	while	consequently	nevertheless
as well as	then	therefore	in spite of
not only ... but also	at first	for this reason	on the other hand
The heavy elephant fell into the well **and** sank.	**When** his friends heard the splash, they ran to help.	The elephant sank like a stone **because** he was heavy.	**Despite** all their efforts, his friends could not save him.

Certain types of connectives are features of different types of text. For example:

Narrative texts often use time connectives to sequence the story:

> *Just then, the gate opened to reveal a magic garden.*

Explanatory texts often use cause connectives:

> *The rock melts **because** it is so hot.*

Discussion texts often use opposition connectives:

> ***Nevertheless,** a new shopping centre will create jobs.*

(20 marks)

Find the connectives in the sentences.

1   Although there was a lot of thunder last night,
    it didn't wake my brother up.

2   We enjoyed our holiday in Spain despite the fact that it rained half the time.

3   Grandad has retired now. Before that he was an electrician in Newcastle.

4   Don't buy those shoes, Ashra. They're too expensive. Besides they're too big
    for you.

5   Megan is no good at netball. However, she is a very good tennis player.

6   He wants to play for our team since we are the champions.

7   Mum says we can go to Paul's party as well as go swimming.

8   Dad turned off the TV because of all the lightning.

9   Ella didn't give up until she had completed the course.

10 The competition will be held on Saturday unless the weather is bad.

**Choose the right words from the brackets. Make sure that you choose words
that fit the punctuation of each sentence.**

11 Mary finished her homework (then, and then) she phoned her friend.

12 Peter did not want to go out. The wind was bitterly cold. (Beside, Besides),
    he wanted to watch his favourite programme on television.

13 John decided not to go fishing with his brother. (Instead, Afterwards) he
    regretted his decision.

14 I'm looking forward to going to my new school because several of my
    friends are going too. (However, In addition,) it is not far from my home,
    (so, consequently) I shall be able to walk there.

15 Some people do not eat a certain type of meat. (However, For example,)
    Muslims do not eat pork, (or, and) Hindus do not eat beef. Vegetarians,
    (surprisingly, of course,) do not eat any kind of meat.

16 Two lorries collided and left a large pool of oil on the road, (therefore, so)
    the road was closed for nearly two hours (while, meanwhile) men used
    chemicals to remove the oil.

Put suitable linking words in the spaces below. You can choose words from the list below or use your own. Put in capital letters where necessary. *(20 marks)*

so that	while	nevertheless	in addition	although	
since	because of	instead of	in spite	after	moreover
therefore	however	before	furthermore	consequently	

1   It is very difficult for me to concentrate on my homework _____ somebody is watching a noisy programme on television.

2   Many people have to live in a single room or a small flat _____ the high price of houses.

3   Adam is only allowed to play outside _____ he has done his homework.

4   Driving a high-speed train must be interesting and exciting. _____ , it can also be rather dangerous at times.

5   Our house is not far from a river, so it could flood when we have a long period of heavy rain. _____, we prefer to stay here and have no wish to move.

6   Paul had to walk to school yesterday _____ the bus-drivers were on strike.

7   We receive a lot of rubbish emails, so we delete most of them _____ reading them.

8   Dad has bought a new bedside clock _____ he won't be late for work again.

9   Moira likes to play the piano _____ she has never had any lessons.

10 Many immigrants have come to Britain because it is easier for them to find a job here. _____, the rate of pay and the living conditions are better than those in their own country.

What connectives of similar meaning can be used instead of the words in bold?

11 I doubt whether our team will win on Saturday **because** our forwards haven't scored a goal in the past five games. **Besides**, our defence is weak.

12 **Before long**, we will need some new players **since** the existing ones are under-performing.

13 **For this reason**, we are bottom of the league, **despite** the manager's efforts,

14 **Following** a fight, Butler was booked. **So**, we were a man down.

15 **As long as** the players carry on like this, we won't win. **Also**, our sponsorship will be at stake.

Sometimes there are alternative words that we can use to link statements. In the following sentences, which words in the brackets *cannot* be used in each space?
(10 marks)

1 _____ having only ten men for most of the game, Chelsea won 2–1 (However, Despite, In spite of)

2 Miss Johnson is not opposed to the change in the rules. _____ she is strongly in favour of the change. (On the other hand, Nevertheless, On the contrary)

3 We're not sure _____ our cousins are coming on Saturday or not. (that, whether, if)

4 Kate is a fast and skilful netball player. _____ she can play in any position. (Moreover, Furthermore, Subsequently)

5 Boil the eggs for three minutes _____ take them out of the water. (then, and then, but first)

6 You are not yet 14 _____ you are not old enough to take part in the competition. (Therefore, Beside, Although)

7 Paul went to buy some bread _____ there was none left at home. (because, since, as)

8 John locked the door and turned off the light. _____ he discovered that everybody had not yet come home. (Moreover, Subsequently, Afterwards)

9 Sue inadvertently touched the hot pan. _____ she burned her hand. (For example, Consequently, Similarly)

10 The postman comes to our house every day _____ the weather. (whatever, despite, instead of)

Use the information in each pair of sentences to make one sentence linked by a connective. *(10 marks – 2 marks for each correct sentence)*

11 This is the house. We used to live here.

12 Our family grew very big. The house became too small for us.

13 My parents bought a new house. It was very expensive.

14 We hired a lorry. We could move everything ourselves and reduce the cost.

15 Paul hurt his left arm. He was helping to lift the piano into the lorry.

Forming complex sentences 1

🔑 Key idea

Complex sentences are made up of more than one clause. The clauses can be joined in different ways. Here are some examples:

- **Use the –ing form of a verb (a participle).**

    Jumping off the trampoline, I fell and hurt myself.
    *Mary got on the bus, **thinking** that it was going to London.*

    Note that a comma is used to separate the two clauses.
    Do not use a comma if the –ing verb gives information about the word immediately before it:

    *Mary got on the bus **going** to London.*

- **Use a conjunction.**

    *The boy was frightened **because** he was alone.*
    ***Although** he was frightened, the boy did not show it.*

- **Use a relative pronoun.**

    *Carl, **who** is only ten, is an excellent cello player.*

Try it out! •

Say which sentences need a comma and which do not. Rewrite the ones that do, punctuating them correctly. *(10 marks)*

1   Anita opened the box thinking that it was empty.

2   Phil picked up the wallet lying on the pavement.

3   I started to put on a shoe believing that it was mine.

4   Melissa opened the door leading to the back garden.

5   Sunita started to put on the shoes lying by her bed.

6   Joseph opened the door not realising that his father was painting the other side of it.

7   I picked up the wallet wondering whether the owner's name was inside it.

8   A traffic warden put a ticket on all the cars blocking the road.

9   We watched some men repairing a leak in a water pipe.

10 Gordon sat in a cell at the police station bitterly regretting his night out.

Keep practising! •

Use the information in each pair of sentences to make one sentence starting with the given word. You can change, add or omit words where necessary. Make sure you punctuate correctly! *(10 marks)*

1   (**After**) We finished lunch. Mary and I cleared the table.

2   (**After**) The dentist took a tooth out. Paul's mouth felt numb for hours.

3   (**Although**) Cows are big animals. They do not normally attack people.

4   (**Although**) Ice-cream and chocolate may not be very good for you. I like them both.

5   (**Despite**) Scotland can be a very chilly place. We are very happy living there.

6   (**Despite**) John is not very tall. He is an excellent soccer player.

7   (**Because of**) There is ice on the road. It has been closed to traffic.

8   (**Because of**) Crocodiles have a very thick skin. They are not easily injured.

9   (**Before**) We went to bed. We turned off all the lights.

10 (**Before**) Ranjeet checked the brakes on his bike. He went for a ride with his friend.

Take up the challenge! •

Complete the sentences in any sensible way. *(10 marks)*

1   What's the name of the girl who _____?

2   The player who _____ used to go to our school.

3   What have you done with the video that _____?

4   The shop that _____ is a complete wreck, so it will have to be rebuilt.

5   The police are trying to find out who _____.

6   Did you ever find out the name of the woman whose _____?

7   The team which _____ will go through to the final.

8   The candidate whom _____ has won the election.

9   The answer that _____ was different from mine.

10 Can you please tell me what _____?

Punctuation

 Key idea

Adding clauses increases the complexity of sentences, so more punctuation is needed.

Full stops are used to mark the end of sentences that are statements.
- Use a full stop to separate two main clauses or use a connective to join them.
  - ✗ *Paul repaired his bicycle, then he went for a ride.*
  - ✓ *Paul repaired his bicycle. Then he went for a ride.* **or**
  - ✓ *Paul repaired his bicycle and then (he) went for a ride.*
- A subordinate clause cannot be punctuated as if it is a main clause.
  - ✗ *Paul went for a ride with his friend.* **When** *he had repaired his bicycle.*
  - ✓ *Paul went for a ride with his friend* **when** *he had repaired his bicycle.*
- Use a full stop (and **not** a question mark) after an indirect question.
  - ✗ *The woman asked me where the railway station is?*
  - ✓ *The woman asked me where the railway station is.*

Colons are used to make the reader pause and to give more information about words before the colon:
> *Dad grows several kinds of vegetables: carrots, beans, peas and broccoli.*
> *When the door opened, we had a nasty surprise: a huge gorilla stood there.*

Semi-colons are used:
- to link two sentences of equal importance about the same subject:
  > *Some people love coffee; others dislike it.*
- when some of the items in a list already need a comma:
  > *Paul collects lots of stamps: ones of ships, both old and new; airmail stamps, especially from the USA; Christmas stamps and many others.*

Apostrophes are used to show:
- omission: *I'm afraid we can't come before two o'clock.*
- possession: *The ladies' coats are here, but the men's coats are in my sister's room.*

Commas, brackets and dashes are used to separate explanatory words and phrases.
> *The story of Oliver Twist, a poor orphan, was written by Dickens.*
> *The story of Oliver Twist (a poor orphan) was written by Dickens.*
> *The story of Oliver Twist – a poor orphan – was written by Dickens*

Put in full stops and capital letters where necessary. *(10 marks)*

1   please give this book to mike when you see him it is from his uncle in wales

2   we put all our bags in the boot of the car then we set off on our journey, looking forward to visiting our relatives in cornwall

3   although the crowd was very noisy and shouted insults at some of the visiting players, there was no serious disturbance this was a pleasant surprise for the police

4   that's Kate's brother come and meet him he plays in goal for his school team

5   sri lanka is an island country off the southern tip of india it used to be called ceylon

6   "thanks for the camera," kate said to her uncle "it will be very useful"

7   the woman asked me what my name is and where I live

8   i'm not sure how much margaret paid for her new bicycle

9   you can throw those old shoes away they're no good now

10   we waited a few minutes then we went round to the back of the house.

Rewrite these sentences, putting in a colon or a semi-colon where necessary. Write "no change" if additional punctuation is not necessary. *(10 marks – 2 marks for each correct sentence)*

11   Use two of these words in your own sentences through, across, around, into, beyond.

12   The traffic in front of us came to a halt we guessed that there had been an accident.

13   That cat is not ours it belongs to one of our neighbours.

14   Mrs Wilson glanced at the items on her shopping list milk, tea, sugar, cereal and fruit.

15   My father is a pilot and often flies to France, Spain, Germany, Denmark and Sweden.

(20 marks)

Put in apostrophes where they are needed. In each case say whether the apostrophe is for omission or possession.

1 Is this Marys book or yours?

2 Hurry up! The games starting in five minutes time.

3 Mum will be back in ten minutes. Shes gone to get Grandmas medicine.

4 Theres a smell of burning coming from the neighbours house.

5 Lets pick some of Peters strawberries; Im sure he wont mind.

6 Which painting do you prefer: Pauls or Annes?

7 Sheila makes childrens clothes and sells them whenever theres a market.

8 Whos hiding in the back of the plumbers van?

9 Those shoes are not Mikes. They must be somebody elses.

10 The peoples reaction to the three judges decision isnt going to be good.

Punctuate the sentences below, using capital letters, full stops, commas, question marks, exclamation marks, speech marks and apostrophes as appropriate.

11 mrs collins the librarian told us to be quiet

12 her colourful mexican hat had red green blue and yellow stripes on it

13 ahmed broke through the winners tape at the end of the race, shouting im the champion

14 encouraged by the crowds shouts the players who hadnt won a game for weeks were spurred on to victory

15 when my grannys teeth fell into her soup we shrieked with laughter

16   wont you please turn that noise down pleaded my dad

17   since the new puppys arrival theres never a dull moment in our house

18   the tiger which had escaped from the zoo was stalking Anns pony

19   i dont believe it she gasped theres an elephant sitting on my car

20   doesnt your friend live near buckingham palace in london

Take up the challenge! •

Which words in these sentences can be put inside commas, brackets or dashes? Rewrite the sentences deciding which method to use each time. *(20 marks – 2 marks for each correctly written sentence)*

1   We hired a boat and went fishing about half a mile from the shore. Later on unaware of the approaching storm we moved to a site further away from the beach.

2   Hanya asked her friends two boys and two girls to complete her questionnaire.

3   One problem with our new house but not by any means the only problem is that it has practically no garden.

4   When you see Donna, tell her but not her brother about the party.

5   The game in Madrid starts at 10 a.m. 9 o'clock our time so don't get up late if you want to watch it on TV tomorrow.

6   Tomorrow the court will hear the evidence of Tim Williams the main witness for the prosecution before the defendant is called to the stand.

7   If you can type and even if you can't you will find that a computer is very useful for obtaining all sorts of information.

8   When the man was taken to the police station, he was charged with being disorderly which he admitted and with assaulting a police officer which he denied.

9   The price of petrol like many other things has risen steadily in recent years.

10   When you go to the office, ask for Miss Ellis the chief executive's personal secretary and explain the problem or the most important part of it to her.

Assessment 1

Word class quiz

Give one-word answers. *(5 marks – 0.5 mark for each correct answer)*

1. Which proper noun is the name of the capital of Spain?
2. Which adjective is the opposite of "boring"?
3. Which pronoun is the plural of both "himself" and "herself"?
4. Which noun is the name we give to people who listen to a sermon in church?
5. Which adverb is also the name of a place where people can get water?
6. Which adjective is the opposite of "smallest"?
7. Which preposition can be used with the meaning "from one end to the other end" (of a tunnel)?
8. Which connective can mean "in addition"?
9. What is the past participle of the verb "begin"?
10. What is the present participle of the verb "die"?

Make a choice 1

Choose the right word or letter each time. *(5 marks – 0.5 mark for each correct answer)*

1. The storm was bad in the afternoon but even (worse, worst) during the night.
2. The letter "h" is (silence, silent) at the beginning of some words.
3. Be careful! We are approaching (a, an) S-bend which is known to be dangerous.
4. Many pupils study (a, an) European language at their secondary school.
5. A plum is usually bigger (than, then) a cherry.
6. The letter ("b", "p") is not pronounced in "cupboard" and "raspberry".
7. We haven't finished cutting the grass (or, nor) pulling up the weeds yet.
8. When the driver was charged with being drunk in charge of a vehicle, he could not say (anything, nothing) to the police officer.
9. Scientists say that global warming will have a big (affect, effect) on our climate.
10. This is a present for Mum from Mike and (me, I).

Make a choice 2

Choose the right word each time. X means that no word is needed. *(5 marks – 0.5 mark for each correct answer)*

1   We haven't seen David (for, since) at least a fortnight ago.

2   Did your brother get through his driving test (successful, successfully)?

3   Look! That poor dog has hurt one of (it's, its) paws.

4   Don't forget the old saying: "(Practice, Practise) makes perfect."

5   My uncle's new house is better than (ours, ours', our's).

6   There (is, are) a surprising number of mistakes in that letter.

7   The number of cases of tuberculosis in Britain (has, have, is) increased in recent years.

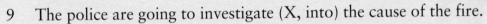

8   When we strolled (passed, past) Mr Jordan's shop, we were surprised to find that (they, it, X) was closed.

9   The police are going to investigate (X, into) the cause of the fire.

10 They suspect that it was (cause, caused) by arson, but they don't have any convincing (evidence, evident) yet.

Make a choice 3

Choose the right word each time. *(5 marks – 0.5 mark for each correct answer)*

1   Where were you going when Paul (see, saw, seen) you on a bus yesterday?

2   We didn't break the window. It was (breaked, broke, broken) before.

3   According to the news, a lot of cars are (steal, stole, stolen) in this country and then (sell, selling, sold) abroad.

4   This year I did not (forget, forgot, forgotten) my friend's birthday.

5   During the night, two trees in the school (ground, grounds) were (blowed, blown, blew) down by gale-force winds.

6   We use (a, an) before "X-ray" (and, but) (a, an) before "xylophone"

7   When Mr Wilson went on duty during the storm, he was wearing (a, an) uniform and carrying (a, an) umbrella.

8   You have left (a, an) "r" out of "Mediterranean" and put in (a, an) "u" unnecessarily.

9   (Do, Does) all the gear belong to you, Paul, or is some of it (Mike's, Mikes)?

10 I'm delighted to tell you that the committee (has, have) considered your proposal and given it their blessing.

Make a choice 4

Choose the right word each time. *(10 marks)*

1   Anne ran 60 metres (then, and then) she (past, passed) the baton to the next runner.

2   Yesterday was Wednesday (and therefore, therefore) tomorrow must be (Friday, Tuesday).

3   Ahmed decided to have a sleep after lunch. There was no work for him to do. (Besides, Beside) he could (hard, hardly) keep his eyes open.

4   Erin wanted to watch a film on television at 4 p.m. (Furthermore, However,) she missed (them, it) because she was late getting home.

5   I was (finished, finishing) my homework last night when a bat flew in through the window, (gave, giving) us all an unpleasant surprise.

Using passive verbs

(10 marks – 1 mark for each correct answer)

Put in the *present passive* form of the verbs in brackets. Use *am/is/are* + a past participle.

   Examples: *am (not) invited; is (not) broken; are (not) sold*

Every year our Sports Day (1)_____ (hold) in July. The field (2)_____ (mark) out for races and everyone (3)_____ (give) a chance to show what they can do. Parents (4)_____ (invite) and (5)_____ (often use) as judges.

Put in the *past passive* form of the verbs in brackets. Use *was/were* + a past participle.

   Examples: *was (not) invited; were (not) broken*

Last sports day, the first race (6) _____ (won) by my friend Paul who (7) _____ (wear) his new trainers. The school record (8) _____ (break) and his picture (9)_____ (print) in the local paper. He (10) _____ (give) a special prize by the school governors.

Joining sentences

Use the information in each pair or group of sentences to make one sentence. You can change, add or omit words. *(10 marks – 2 marks for each correct sentence)*

1   These are the best of the photos. Uncle Amos took them with his new camera last summer.

2   Many trains were delayed. There was a severe storm. A large number of buses were delayed too. The storm lasted nearly 48 hours.

3   We put sandbags in front of our door. We hoped that they would stop the water from coming in. They were not completely successful.

4   Anne was playing on the trampoline. She hurt her left leg. That was yesterday. The doctor says the injury is not serious.

5   The shop used to sell fireworks. It has stopped selling them. Parents and the police complained. Very young children were able to buy them.

Punctuating sentences

Punctuate these sentences and put in capital letters where necessary. *(10 marks – 2 marks for each sentence)*

1   Paul checked the email on Marys computer then he turned it off because he wanted to phone his friend and arrange to go fishing with him.

2   Although Sophie is not a strong swimmer she rescued a young girl at the swimming-pool and stayed with her while she recovered then she escorted her home.

3   theres something wrong with the printer mike told his father it wont print check to see if theres any paper in it his father said you may have to put some paper in

4   the notice on the door of mr singhs shop was quite clear closed it said in capital letters open 1–5 p.m. it added in small letters.

5   Dave Burton the captain of our team scored twice in the first half then he pulled a muscle in his left leg so Mr Donald replaced him at half-time by sending on John Lee our reserve striker.

Active and passive verbs 2

🔑 Key idea

Verbs can be in the active or passive voice.

* When we use an active verb, the action goes from the subject to the object.

  ⟶

  David ate some fish and chips.

* When we use a passive verb, the action goes from the verb back to the subject.

  ⟵

  An unlucky surfer was eaten by a hungry shark.

Try it out! •

In the following passage, find five *passive present* verbs and five *passive past* verbs. *(10 marks)*

Before World War II, thousands of cars were produced in Britain. Morris, Ford and Austin cars were regularly exported to countries all over the world, and provided jobs for thousands of workers. The Morris Oxford was invariably used as a taxi because it was spacious and provided plenty of room for passengers in the back of the vehicle.

However, the manufacture of civilian vehicles ceased during the war. Subsequently, fewer vehicles were made in the second half of the twentieth century. Many factories were closed down and employees lost their jobs.

Now fewer cars are manufactured in the United Kingdom. Some Japanese cars are assembled here, but many of their parts are made in Japan or another overseas country. In their place, Japanese, French, Italian and German cars are imported every week. They are advertised on television and have become more popular than British cars.

Put in the *passive present* or *past* form of the verbs in brackets. *(10 marks – 0.5 mark for each correct answer)*

1   In some countries, water _____ (boil) before it _____ (drink) because it may contain harmful bacteria.

2   When there is an earthquake, many buildings _____ (destroy) and hundreds or thousands of people _____ (kill).

3   A fisherman has a hard life. Every year a number of fishermen _____ (lose) at sea when their trawler _____ (sink) by huge waves or _____ (hit) by another vessel.

4   Last week we _____ (invite) to a party which _____ (hold) at our local community centre. We _____ (ask) **not** to bring presents for Katie.

5   My brother works in a factory where various kinds of refrigerators _____ (make). Before each fridge leaves the factory, it _____ (inspect) carefully. It _____ (test) to make sure that it works properly.

6   Ten years ago, this area consisted of fields. Then hundreds of houses _____ (build), a playground _____ (provide) for children and a new health centre _____ (open).

7   Before a fight, both boxers _____ (weigh) to make sure that they are the correct weight. In addition, they _____ (examine) by a doctor to check that they are fit.

8   At the last Olympic Games, several new records _____ (establish) but some athletes _____ (disqualify) for having taken prohibited stimulants.

Take up the challenge! •

Rewrite these sentences. If the sentence is in the active voice, change it to passive. If it is passive, change it to active. *(10 marks – 2 marks for each correct sentence)*

1   Tanya found your watch in the playground this afternoon.
2   The food was cooked by a professional chef.
3   An expert repaired our computer a few days ago.
4   All the passengers on the flight were searched by security officials.
5   The police have arrested two men and taken them to the police station.

Official language

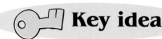 **Key idea**

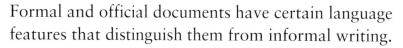

Formal and official documents have certain language features that distinguish them from informal writing.

Informal: first person (personal); colloquial/slang vocabulary; use of contractions; short, simple sentences; exclamations, questions

Formal: third person (impersonal); technical, subject-specific vocabulary; no contractions; complex sentences; statements

After learning about official language at school, Len Benton decided to have some fun with his friend, Mary. She wanted to borrow his bike, so he wrote her an "official" letter on his computer.

Dear Miss Evans

We have been instructed by our client, Mr Len Benton, to communicate directly with you in respect of a proposed short-term lease of his bicycle, Swifto, Mark III, hereinafter referred to as "the machine". It is our understanding that you wish to take temporary possession of the said machine for a period not exceeding seven calendar days.

Our client has agreed to waive his statutory right to require you to insure the machine but stipulates that you indicate your consent to the following conditions:
(1) you will employ your best efforts to ensure that not more than three persons of reasonable weight make use of said machine on one and the same occasion
(2) you will reimburse our client for any adverse structural change, deterioration of parts or other harmful effects sustained during the lease period
(3) you hereby undertake to restore to our client possession of said machine not later than 2000 hours on 15 April next coming by delivering the machine to him in the same excellent condition (rust excepted) as it was when you first took possession of it on 8 April.

Kindly indicate that you consent to the terms of the proposed lease by signing the enclosed copy of this letter and delivering it to us not later than 5 April.

Yours sincerely
(Peter Rabbit) for Snatchem, Grabbit and Keepe

(10 marks)

Find expressions in the letter which have these meanings:

1 write to	3 We believe	5 a week	7 try hard	9 damage
2 loan	4 borrow	6 you agree	8 at one time/together	10 return

Keep practising! •

(10 marks)

Mary's mother saw Len's letter and asked her what it was all about. Pretend that you are Mary. In <u>simple, everyday English</u>, tell your mother the contents of the letter.

Take up the challenge! • • • • • • • • • • • • • • • • • • •

(10 marks)

Using simple English, say what these expressions mean:

1   Please be advised that …

2   It is our considered opinion that …

3   Do you undertake to reimburse us in the event of any loss on our part?

4   The agreement will terminate on …

5   His account of the event is substantially at variance with the facts.

6   He was driving in a manner which displayed a wanton disregard for other road-users.

7   His land is likely to command a substantial sum if sold at auction.

8   He was accused of removing goods from the store without paying for them.

9   She is a young lady who holds an exceptionally high opinion of herself.

10 In a library, you must refrain from communicating with others orally.

Forming complex sentences 2

🔑 Key idea

Complex sentences are made up of more than one clause.

| subordinate clause | main clause | subordinate clause |

When she went upstairs, *the princess couldn't sleep* because a pea was in her bed.

There are different types of subordinate clauses. They are linked to the main clause with connectives.

- **Adverbial clauses** do the work of adverbs.

    *Paul went to bed **when** he was tired.*
    *Karla was hungry **because** she had not eaten lunch.*
    *The taxi stopped **where** two roads meet.*

- **Adjectival clauses** do the work of adjectives.

    *My father, **who** is a very skilful mechanic, will soon repair your bike.*
    *This is the road **that** was built in Roman times.*
    *The cable **which** leads to the rear wheel is broken.*

- **Noun clauses** take the place of nouns.
    They can be the subject or object in a main clause:
    subject:
    with a noun: *The **cause** of the fire is a mystery.*
    with a noun clause: ***How it started** is a mystery.*
    object:
    with a noun: *I don't know his **address**.*
    with a noun clause: *I don't know **where** he lives.*

*A **main clause** is like the trunk of a tree.*
It is the most important part.
***Subordinate clauses** are like branches.*
They cannot live by themselves.
They need a main clause to cling to.

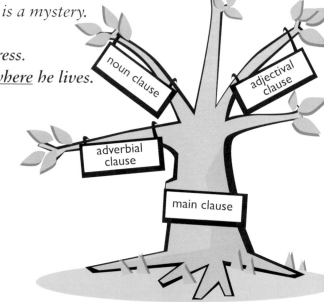

(20 marks)

Write out the *main clause* in each of these sentences.

1   Our game was cancelled because there was a thunderstorm.

2   Although my father is over forty, he still plays football for a local team.

3   What's the name of the player who scored both the goals?

4   Our dog barks whenever the postman comes to our house.

5   The grass has turned brown because we haven't had enough rain.

6   The bus that passes our house takes me straight to school.

7   If you go to bed late, you will probably feel tired the next day.

8   The watch, which is quite valuable, belongs to Sarjit Singh.

9   The bus was full, so it did not stop at our bus stop.

10   Until everyone is ready, the starter won't fire his gun.

Write out the *subordinate clause* in each of these sentences.

11   Anybody who is caught stealing from a shop may be sent to prison.

12   My mother always leaves some windows open
so that we get enough fresh air.

13   Everybody who knows Mary Wilson says
she is a very kind and unselfish girl.

14   As soon as the water boils, add the pasta.

15   Sue hid her money where nobody else
would ever think of looking.

16   What have you done with the book that
I borrowed from the library?

17   Everybody whose name I read out has
volunteered to take part in our
school play.

18   Once Sadie had learned to swim, there was no stopping her!

19   Switch your mobile phone off when you go into the hospital.

20   The team for which Tom plays has been knocked out of the competition.

(20 marks)

Think of a connective to fill the gap in each sentence. Make sure the connective you choose is logical and fits the meaning of the sentence.

1   _____ you want to go with us, you must be ready in five minutes.

2   No one expected our team to win _____ they'd not won a game all season.

3   _____ the shopkeeper lowered his prices, his sales increased.

4   He tried his best _____ it wasn't good enough.

5   _____ the problem, you can count on me to help.

6   They came to a stop _____ the road forked in three directions.

7   We could hear perfectly _____ we were in the last row.

8   The candidate, _____ campaigned tirelessly, unfortunately lost.

9   _____ I received the hoax phone call, I notified the police.

10   The city _____ I love the most is Paris.

Combine each pair of sentences to make one complex sentence with a main clause and a subordinate clause. Try to use as many different connecting words as you can.

11   The referee will blow his whistle. The players will leave the field.

12   I want to get the autograph of that player. He scored the winning goal.

13   What caused the accident? The police are trying to find that out.

14   You bought some ice cream last week. What was the name of it?

15   There may be a drought. Then water will be rationed.

16   Mel put a stamp on the envelope. Then she posted it.

17   How much does a mobile phone cost? Samir wants to know that.

18   That's the boy. His father used to be a boxer.

19   There was dense fog this morning. There were a number of minor accidents.

20   Show me the photos. You took them during the holidays.

Take up the challenge

Write your own clauses that could end these sentences. Say whether the clause you wrote is a main clause or a subordinate clause. *(10 marks)*

1 The committee could not agree, so

2 Unless the weather is bad

3 Whatever you say

4 Encouraged by his coach

5 Our teacher said we could have a disco

6 So that no one gets hurt

7 We waited ages for the taxi

8 Whenever I feel afraid

9 Joseph was sleeping soundly

10 Before we had time to think

Draw a grid like the one below. For each sentence write the main clause, the subordinate clause and what type of subordinate clause it is: adverbial, adjectival or noun. The grid has some examples to help you. *(10 marks – 2 marks for each correct answer)*

Main clause	Subordinate clause	Subordinate clause type
I don't know	where he lives	noun
The bus was full	so it did not stop for us	adverbial
This is the watch	that my mother gave me	adjectival

11 Although Susan is not very tall, she is a very fast runner.

12 I know the woman who won the lottery jackpot.

13 Call me when you are ready to leave.

14 We told the woman what she wanted to know.

15 Don't eat the cheese that I bought for the party.

Making notes

 **Key idea**

We make notes to extract the most important points from written words (such as information text) or spoken words (such as a telephone conversation or interview). We write them down in a shorter form.

How we make notes depends on why we are making them and who they are for.

- If we are making notes for our own use, we can use shorthand, contractions, abbreviated words, symbols, diagrams – or any method we like – as long as we can understand our own notes!
- If we are making notes for other people, we need to ensure the information relevant to them is in the notes.

 Top Tip

Notes do not need to be in complete sentences.

Try it out! •

You have your own calendar or diary at home. What note will you write down for each of these situations? *(10 marks)*

1   Your best friend's birthday is on the twenty-first of November.

2   Your mother says, "I've made a dental appointment for you for at 1030 on the first of August."

3   Your father says, "We're all going to Spain for a holiday from the sixth to the fourteenth of August. We will need to leave by noon."

4   A sister says, "Sue is having a party on May the tenth. You're invited. The party will be from five in the afternoon until nine at night in Room 3 of the Memorial Hall in Market Street."

5   Your mother says, "I've just made an appointment for you to see an optician at half past four in the afternoon on June the sixth to see if you need glasses."

Keep practising! ●●●●●●●●●●●●●●●●●●●●●●●●●●●●●●

While you are babysitting for a neighbour, you receive these phone calls. What notes can you make to help you write the messages for your neighbour? *(10 marks)*

1   This is Doris from Newton Motors. Please tell Mrs Jackson that her car is ready for collection. We're open every day from eight in the morning until eight at night. She can collect it any time.

2   Oh, I really wanted to speak to Mrs Jackson. She has an appointment to see Dr Jordan on the eighth of March at half past nine in the morning, but Dr Jordan won't be available, so I've changed the appointment to a quarter past ten on the morning of the tenth of March. If that's not convenient, please ask her to ring me at 094-384 By the way, I'm Sally Enright.

Take up the challenge! ●●●●●●●●●●●●●●●●●●●●●●●●●●

You are P.C. Williams. You receive the following information by phone. Take notes of the important points that need to be dealt with. *(10 marks)*

1   Hallo. My name's Tom Logan. There's just been a serious accident on the M99, about two miles south of junction 38 A lorry has collided with a petrol tanker, and they've both caught fire. The road is blocked in both directions. Two cars have run into the wreckage. I'm sure somebody has been killed or seriously injured. You'd better send a couple of ambulances and tell the fire brigade. It looks a horrible mess. Traffic is at a standstill. It's one big muddle. We need help.

2   This is Cynthia Marsden. I live at 48 Larch Street. There's something very strange going on at the back of 44 Larch Street. I'm looking out of the window and I can see a couple of men – well, it might be a man and a woman, I'm not sure – in the back garden. They're both carrying bags. Now they're doing something at the back door. Oh! They've opened it and gone inside. But I know the people who live there. They're on holiday in Ireland right now, so the house must be empty. Oh, wait a minute. They're coming out. One of them is carrying a TV set to a van parked in the lane behind our houses. The other has two bags full of something. I'm sure they're burglars, so you'd better send somebody straightaway.

Writing a summary

🔑 Key idea

A summary is a re-telling in a shorter number
of words of something you have read or heard.
- Summaries require writing in complete sentences.
- Summaries should include the main idea and important details only.

Try it out! •

**Start by shortening just a group of words. In each case, give one word that
summarises the group of words below.** *(10 marks)*

1   a place where crops are grown or cattle are raised

2   the House of Commons and the House of Lords together

3   a group of pupils taught together in one room in a school

4   something you can give a person at Christmas or on his or her birthday

5   a lot of people close together (on a beach or in a town)

6   go up or become greater (in price or number)

7   (go) from one end to the other end (of a pipe or hole)

8   a large group of musicians who follow their conductor

9   a number of players who play a game together as one unit

10 all our warships and sailors together

Keep practising! •

**Read each statement. Then say whether each headline after it is an appropriate
summary or not.** *(10 marks)*

1   Government minister: "As you all know, I am strongly against raising taxes
normally and all in favour of reducing them. However, on this occasion, I
would agree to a modest increase in order to improve our National Health
Service."

a) Minister favours tax increase. c) Minister knocks National Health Service.
b) Minister strongly opposed to tax increases.

2 Member of Parliament: "Corporal punishment should be brought back to deal with school bullies, young hooligans and anybody who seeks to disrupt orderly education in schools. There is a great deal of truth in the old saying: 'Spare the rod and spoil the child'."
a) Bullying increases in schools.   c) MP knocks education in schools.
b) MP calls for stricter discipline.

3 Newspaper article: "When a ship laden with wooden planks hit rocks off the Cornish coast, waves washed the timber ashore. The insurance company abandoned the cargo and it was soon removed by grateful locals."
a) Bonus for DIY home-owners.   c) Company abandons local people.
b) Police to tackle wreckers.   d) Looters sweep the beach clean.

Take up the challenge! •

Make a summary of each of the following in one sentence of not more than 15 words. *(10 marks – 2½ marks for each appropriate summary)*

1 Pope John Paul II suffered from Parkinson's disease for some years. He became seriously ill early in 2005 but survived bravely until April 2005, when he died peacefully in Rome.

2 Last month Mary was unlucky and caught influenza a few days before her tenth birthday. As a result, she was in bed for three days and absent from school for nearly a week.

3 A boy hurt his left ankle during a football game yesterday. However, he stayed on the field and helped his team win 2–1 The boy was Paul's brother and he was hurt when an opponent kicked him accidentally.

4 Some time next month, we shall be leaving our present home. For a number of reasons, my parents have bought a house about a mile from where we live now, so we will move to the Linford area. That suits all of us since the new house is much nearer my school and most of my friends, so I am very happy about the move.

Mary hit by flu epidemic   **Injured footballer battles on**

Happy house move for local family

Editing

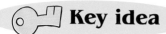

Key idea

Editing involves reviewing and improving our own (or someone else's) writing to make it more effective.

A checklist for editing
- ✓ Check that text is appropriate for **audience** and **purpose**.
- ✓ Check and improve **length** and **layout**.
- ✓ Check and improve **vocabulary**.
- ✓ Check and correct **grammar** and **punctuation**.
- ✓ Check and correct **spelling**.

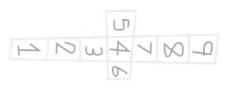

Try it out!

Edit these sentences by correcting punctuation mistakes. *(10 marks)*

1 Paul found a watch in the playground, it looked like his friend's, so he went to find him.

2 "Dave," Paul said. "Is this yours? I was going to take it to the school office, but I thought I'd better ask you first."

3 David was astonished because he had not even noticed that his watch was missing, he looked at his wrist, then he took the watch and examined it carefully.

4 "Yes, its definitely mine," David said. "where did you find it? I don't remember taking it off."

5 "In the playground," Paul told him. "It was lying on the ground near Miss Smiths car. Have you been near her car this morning."

6 "I'm not sure," David said. "Ah Now I remember," he added. "We were playing a game near the cars, and John grabbed me by the arm. It must have come off then"

Keep practising!

Edit these sentences by correcting any spelling and grammar mistakes. *(10 marks – 0.5 mark for each correct answer)*

1 Remind them boys to bring there football jerseys with them tomorrow.

2 It was cold at the begining of the month, but the weather improve gradually.

3 Can you remember Sue's adress? Unfortunately, I've forgot it.

4 Builders is going to develope land next to our playing-field soon.

5 The new "Dr Who" series is quiet imaginative and exiting.

6 Mum and Dad have went to a funeral, so we can't go out untill they return.

7 Mr Parker is a police sergant and sometimes gives evidence at a trail.

8 When you buy a new camera, get a receit and a guarrantee.

9 Look at those mischievious little kittens playing with their mother's tale.

10 Yesterday, Mary feels slightly embarassed when she fell down the stairs.

Take up the challenge!

Edit this description of one child's day by correcting any mistakes and by using better words where they will improve the article. *(10 marks)*

My busy day

My father is in the Army, so he is oversees now. My mother work in a local nursing home.

Yesterday she had to worked from midnight till 8 a.m., so she was not yet home when I waked up. I got out from bed at 730 and got washed, then I put my clothes on and got my breakfast. After that, I walked to school with one of my freind.

We had lesons in the morning and afternoon. I had lunch at school, it was quite nice because I was very hungry. When I returned to home, I worked in the garden for about an our. I enjoy gardening when the whether is fine. When I had finished in the garden, I went in and did some homework. After that, my mother said that supper was ready. I felt full up after supper, so I sat down at our computer and replied some emails from friends. Next I watched part of a film on television.

At about 10 p.m., I was very tired so I washed and went to bed. Yesterday was a very busy day for me.

Conditional sentences

🔑 Key idea

A conditional sentence says that one thing depends on another. Conditional sentences usually contain the words **if** or **unless**. The "if" or "unless" part of the sentence is a special type of subordinate clause called a **conditional clause**.

> subordinate clause   main clause
>
> *If it rains, the match will be cancelled.*

These are some of the common patterns of conditional sentences:

Habitual (usual) actions

If + *Simple Present* tense, + *Simple Present* tense.
If dogs see a cat, they usually chase it.
If people are tickled, they usually laugh.

Possible or likely actions

If + *Simple Present* tense, + *Simple Future* tense
If you ride more carefully, you won't fall off your bike again.
If Fred campaigns harder, he will win.

Unlikely or impossible actions

If + *Simple Past* tense, + *Present Conditional* tense
If motorists drove more carefully, there would be fewer accidents.
If there were no water, how would we survive?

Past actions that might have happened but did not

If + *Past Perfect* tense, + would/could/might have
If we had had a full team, we would have won.
If you hadn't tickled him, he wouldn't have laughed.

ALERT
Look out for sentences containing **provided that** and **as long as**. They could also be conditional sentences!

 Top Tip
If the conditional clause comes after the main clause, a comma is not needed.

Make conditional sentences by matching a sentence beginning in the left-hand column with words from the right-hand column. *(15 marks)*

1 Most plants soon die	a) if you don't keep it in a fridge.
2 Fish goes bad quite quickly	b) it tries to catch it.
3 A kettle full of water boils	c) we will have to walk to school.
4 Iron and steel expand	d) if there is ice on it.
5 Snow soon melts	e) if anybody rings the bell on our door.
6 If we make too much noise,	f) if you don't water them.
7 If you put compost on plants,	g) we'd better get a larger pair.
8 If the bus-drivers are on strike,	h) it wastes water.
9 If you leave a tap running,	i) if you heat them.
10 If a cat sees a mouse,	j) rinse your mouth with hot salty water.
11 Workmen put sand on the road	k) if you heat it.
12 If those shoes are too small now,	l) you get much better results.
13 If you've got toothache,	m) if you try to climb over it.
14 That fence will collapse	n) if the sun comes out.
15 Our dog starts to bark	o) our neighbours start to complain.

Make up some funny conditional sentences of your own. Choose five expressions from the left-hand column and add your own ending. *(5 marks)*

Example: *Plants soon die if you sing to them.*

(20 marks)

Choose the right words from the brackets.

1   Keep away from bare or broken electricity cables. If you touch one, you (would, could) be electrocuted.

2   If there is no electricity at your school, the pupils (may, would) be sent home early.

3   Take your mobile phone with you. If there is any kind of emergency, you (would, will) be able to get in touch with us.

4   Most of us agree that if we were lucky enough to win the lottery, we (will, would) share the money with all the members of our family and perhaps we (will, might) give some to charity too.

5   The phone company has cut off Mr Brown's phone and will not reconnect it unless he (paid, pays) his bill and a reconnection charge. If you (are, were) Mr Brown, what (will, would) you do?

6   That cut may become infected if you (didn't, don't) cover it. You (could, will) be sorry if harmful germs get into it.

7   If fishermen from all countries caught as many fish as they (like, liked), soon there (are, would be) no fish left in the sea.

8   If you had put any more tins on that shelf, it (might have, would) collapsed.

9   If it had rained yesterday, you would (be, have been) soaked because you (don't, didn't) an umbrella with you.

10 If more people (use, used) public transport, there (will, would) be less congestion on the roads.

11 If Britain had lost World War II, what (will, would have) happened to my grandparents?

12 If we (live, lived) nearer to school, I (would, could) not have to get up so early.

Put in the right form of the verbs in brackets. *(9 marks)*

Mr Trant drove round a bend and saw a tree across the road. He put on his brakes and just managed to stop in time.

1   If Mr Trant (not stop) in time, he would have hit the tree. The people in the car might (kill).

2   If Mr Trant had not been alert, he would (hit) the tree.

3   If Mr Trant had been drunk, he might (have) a serious accident.

4   If the tree (fall) on Mr Trant's car, he could (get) a headache.

5   There would have been no danger if the tree (not fall) across the road.

6   If Mr Trant (take) a different route, there (be) no problem.

Make up a conditional sentence for each of the three situations about things that did not happen in the past. *(6 marks – 2 marks for each sentence)*

Example: *Paul went to bed late last night. His mother did not call him this morning. He woke up late and was late for school.*

If Paul's mother had called him this morning, he would not have been late for school.

7   Tom went to buy some fish and chips but he could not get any because the shop was closed.

8   Anne was late for school because the bus broke down, so she had to walk more than two miles in the rain.

9   At the seaside, a raft capsized and two small children fell into the water. A lifeguard saw them and swam towards them. Susan also saw them. The lifeguard saved one child. Susan saved the other child. Neither of the children could swim.

Complete each of these sentences. You can make them serious or funny. *(5 marks)*

10 I were a billionaire, _____

11 If I could make a new law, _____

12 If I were in charge of this school, _____

13 If I were the Prime Minister, _____

14 If I saw a spaceship land in my garden, _____

Assessment 2

From active to passive

Change these sentences so that they contain passive verbs instead of active ones. Leave out the underlined words in your passive sentences.

(5 marks – 0.5 mark for each correct sentence)

1 <u>Some mechanics</u> are repairing our car today.

2 <u>Two men</u> were still repairing the car at half past five.

3 <u>Several people</u> praised Leah for her bravery in rescuing a drowning child.

4 <u>An unknown motorist</u> damaged Miss Fisher's car in a car park yesterday.

5 Traffic accidents injure many people each month.

6 A major fire has damaged the factory opposite Ravi's home.

7 <u>Construction workers</u> have built several new houses on land near our school.

8 <u>Mrs Evans</u> has chosen Linda to play netball for our school team.

9 The police say <u>they</u> will soon catch the two robbers.

10 <u>We</u> will arrest the men and charge <u>them</u> with assault and robbery.

Choosing verb forms

Choose the right words from the brackets. *(10 marks)*

1 Did Mary show you the keys which she _____ (was found, found, is finding) yesterday? She _____ (think, thinks, is thinking) of taking them to the police.

2 Thank you very much for the letter which I _____ (have received, received) two days ago. I am sorry to be slow in replying but I _____ (have been, am, been) very busy for the past few days.

3 Several different types of television sets _____ (are making, made, are made) in Britain. In addition, sets _____ (imported, import, are imported) from other countries.

4 We would be grateful if you _____ please_____ (will ... answer, would ... reply) to our letter as soon as you (able, may, can).

5 My cousin _____ (get, getting, is getting) married next Saturday. More than 250 guests _____ (have invited, have been invited, are inviting).

Joining sentences

Use the information in each group of sentences to make one sentence each time. Do not add "and" or "but". You can change, add or omit words. *(10 marks)*

1 Claire did not like the taste of the medicine. She managed to swallow two spoonfuls of it.

2 It was getting dark. Charlie switched on the light. It was in the kitchen.

3 Birds avoid the berries of some plants. They know they are poisonous. The berries are very pretty.

4 What's the name of the shop? It's in Bond Road. It sells parts for our printer.

5 That's the man. His car was stolen yesterday. He nearly caught the thief.

6 Ashra won the race. She was wearing tight running shoes borrowed from a friend. She had forgotten to bring her own running shoes.

7 The camera was very expensive. Alex decided not to buy it.

8 My cousin is the manager of a computer company. He has taught us how to use computers. We can research topics for our work at school.

9 The food was extremely hot. We could not eat it immediately. We had to wait a few minutes.

10 The girls said they were tourists. They told us that they were Swiss. They were staying here for a fortnight. They were staying with friends.

Find the main clause

Find the main clause in each sentence. *(10 marks)*

1 Any runner who starts before the gun is fired may be disqualified.

2 Ask the lady what she wants or who she is looking for.

3 That's the shop where we often buy Chinese food.

4 Because of greatly increased demand from China, the price of petrol has reached record heights recently.

5 We're ready to leave as soon as you are.

6 The only reason why you can't enter the competition is your age.

7 You can borrow my book if you like, Sue.

8 Although I live on a farm, I don't know much about farm animals because ours is an arable farm.

9 If those new jeans are too long, Mary, I can easily shorten them for you.

10 The doctor told Peter that he no longer needed to take any medicine.

Making notes

One evening you are babysitting for some neighbours, Mr and Mrs Wilson. While your neighbours are out, there are two telephone calls for them. Read what the callers said. Make notes that you could use to write messages for your neighbours. *(10 marks – 5 marks for each set of notes)*

1   Oh, they're both out? Never mind. This is Janet Middleton, Mary Wilson's mother. I was going to meet my daughter at the usual place for coffee tomorrow morning, but I can't come now because my husband (that's Mary's father) has very painful toothache, so we've made an emergency appointment with our dentist. We'll be going to the dentist in the morning and may have to wait some time before he can fit my husband in. The best thing for me to do is cancel the meeting with my daughter. Please tell her that I'll phone her in the afternoon or evening tomorrow so we can arrange to meet another time. Oh, and tell her not to worry about her father. The toothache is very painful, but it's not a major problem. That's all. Goodbye.

2   Can I speak to Mr Wilson, please? Mr Graham Wilson. Oh, I see. Hmmm. If he returns… Oh, sorry. I'm Tony Ellis of Stockton Ellis, the estate agents. If Mr Wilson returns before 7 p.m., please ask him to phone me at 044-342 If that's not possible, please ask him to phone me at my office tomorrow morning. He knows that number, but you can remind him. It's 084-597 Please tell him that we have found a buyer for his Bank Street property but we need a decision from him as soon as possible. Have you got that? Yes, that's right. Please make sure he gets his message. It's very important. Thanks very much. Bye.

Using connectives

Complete the sentences by putting in one of the words in the box. Use each word once only. *(5 marks – 0.5 mark for each correct sentence)*

if   since   which   unless   so that   when   so
later   before   although   despite   than

1   Ugminster Unicorns will not win the Golden Championship _____ they win both their remaining games.

2   On the other hand, _____ they lose one of the games, they will be runners-up.

3   _____ Hardup Harriers is not a very wealthy club, it has done well in recent years.

4 It has moved steadily up the table _____ it joined the football league.

5 More girls are now playing football _____ was the case twenty or thirty years ago.

6 Football is probably not as dangerous a game as hockey, _____ uses sticks and a hard ball.

7 _____ frequent rainy and overcast weather, football matches are rarely cancelled.

8 Many games take place in the evening _____ they can be shown live on television.

9 Players know what to expect from their opponents _____ the game starts.

10 Sometimes substitutes are sent on the field _____ there are only a few minutes left in a game.

Writing summaries

Write a one-sentence summary of each of the following passages. Each sentence should be no more than 15 words. *(10 marks – 5 marks for each summary)*

1 If you watch Channel 4 on television this evening, you will see a really good film for a change. There's nothing worth watching on the other channels at that time, which doesn't surprise me. Anyway, I just wanted to let you know that the film is all about Scotland: its history, its people, the land and scenery – and its future. I've seen it before, but I'm definitely going to watch it again, and I'm sure you'll enjoy it. The film is at 8 p.m. on Channel 4, so don't miss it!

2 For many years, house martins have arrived at our house towards the end of April. A neighbour says they fly all the way from North Africa, but I am not sure if that is true. It seems a long way to go just to get a free meal. Anyway, around 20–25 April, the little birds return to find mud nests under the eaves of our house. They clean out and repair the nests, if necessary, and then hunt for flies and other insects. They raise a family and then, one day late in September, they gather on nearby telephone or electricity wires and fly off together to warmer lands.

Narrative writing

unit 16

 Key idea

The purpose of a narrative text is to tell a story and to entertain the reader. Narrative texts are characterised by the following features:

- details of people, their actions and the places where the actions occur;
- a problem to be solved, often after a series of events (a plot);
- descriptive and effective vocabulary – adjectives, adverbs, powerful verbs;
- variety of sentence lengths and patterns, with correct punctuation;
- past tense – mainly lst or 3rd person;
- connectives denoting time, change, suspense;
- dialogue.

Pip and his sister

Pip, an orphan, is describing his sister, who brought him up. He has returned late from visiting his parents' grave and knows that there will be trouble.

1   My sister, Mrs Joe Gargery, was more than twenty years older than me and had established a great reputation with the neighbours because she had brought me up "by hand". She had a hard and heavy hand, and was in the habit of laying it upon her husband as well as upon me. She was not a good-looking woman, my sister; and I had

5   a general impression that she must have made Joe Gargery marry her by hand. Joe was a fair man, with curls of flaxen hair on each side of his smooth face and with blue eyes. He was a mild, good-natured, sweet-tempered, easy-going, foolish, dear fellow – a sort of Hercules in strength and weakness. My sister, Mrs Joe, with black hair and eyes, had such a red skin that I wondered whether she washed herself with a nutmeg-grater

10   instead of with soap. She was tall and bony, and wore a coarse apron which was stuck full of pins and needles in front.

Joe's forge adjoined our wooden house. When I ran home from the churchyard, the forge was shut, and Joe was sitting alone in the kitchen. Joe and I being fellow-sufferers, Joe hurried to give me the news as soon as I raised the latch of the door and

15   peeped in.

"Mrs Joe has been out a dozen times, looking for you, Pip," he said. "She's out now.

"Is she?"

"Yes, Pip," said Joe, "and what's worse, she's got Tickler with her."

46

At this dismal news, I twisted the only button on my coat round and round, and
looked miserably at the fire. Tickler was a wax-ended piece of cane, worn smooth by
collision with my sensitive frame.

"Has she been gone long, Joe?" I asked.

"Well," said Joe, glancing at the clock, "she's been out about five minutes, Pip. She's
coming now! Get behind the door and hide behind the towel."

I took the advice. My sister threw the door wide open, and finding an obstruction
behind it immediately used Tickler. Then she picked me up and threw me at Joe who,
glad to get hold of me, stood me behind him and quietly fenced me there with his
great leg.

"Where have you been, you young monkey?" said Mrs Joe, stamping her foot.

"I've only been to the churchyard," I said, crying and rubbing myself.

"Churchyard!" repeated my sister. "If it weren't for me you'd have been to the
churchyard long ago, and stayed there. Who brought you up by hand?"

"You did," I said.

Try it out!

**Read "Pip and his sister" (adapted from *Great Expectations*
by Charles Dickens) and then answer these questions.** *(20 marks)*

1   Does Dickens start his story with an action, speech, or a statement? *(1 mark)*

2   Write out the opening sentence. Underline the main clause(s) once and the
    subordinate clauses(s) twice. *(2 marks)*

3   Give examples from the first three paragraphs of words that help to
    contrast Joe and his wife. Write the adjectives and the nouns they describe.
    (3 marks)

4   Why does Dickens use the verb "peeped" (line 15) instead of "looked"?
    What does the verb "fenced" (line 27) tell us about how Joe feels towards
    Pip? *(2 marks)*

5   Why did Pip say that Joe's news was "dismal"? What other descriptive
    words show how Pip was feeling? *(3 marks)*

6   Suggest suitable adverbs that could be inserted after "I asked" (line 22),
    "repeated my sister" (line 31) and "I said" (line 33) *(3 marks)*

7   "Has she been gone long, Joe?" I asked. Is this an example of direct or reported speech? Rewrite it so that it is the other kind of speech. *(3 marks)*

8   In which person is the story written? How can you tell? What effect does this have on the story? *(3 marks)*

The fun of the fair

1   As we approached the Fair, we could see the glare of the lights reflected in the sky. We could hear the murmur of the crowd and see the coloured bulbs on the stalls. All roads led to the Fair and they were all packed with people. The pungent smell of sizzling hotdogs mixed with sweet candyfloss drifted towards us and pulled us onwards. A path
5   opened in the crowd; we entered and were swallowed up.

Our first visit was to The Haunted House. We sat on a little train with hard, wooden seats, which carried us off into the eerie darkness. Clutching the steel-cold restraining bar, we moved slowly through a long dark tunnel, accompanied by mysterious groans and wailing from inside the walls. Luminous spiders dropped down
10   from the ceiling and brushed us as we passed. Ghostly figures appeared on the line and vanished into the gloom. The exhaust fumes of a nearby machine surrounded us. The bitter flavour of fear coated our tongues and we began to feel that we were on a direct line to some kind of hell.

Keep practising! ●

Read the extract above and answer these questions. *(20 marks)*

1   In which tense and person is the extract written. How can you tell? *(1 mark)*

2   The writer uses all the senses – sight, hearing, smell, touch, and even taste – to describe his setting. For each sense, find at least two descriptive words or phrases in the extract. *(10 marks)*

3   Find the sentence where the author has used a semicolon. Explain why you think the author has used it. *(2 marks)*

4   The author often uses sentences containing two main clauses linked by "and". Find two examples of this structure. *(2 marks)*

5   Suggest three places where you could add an adverb. Write out the three phrases with your adverbs. *(3 marks)*

6   Write a suitable sentence of your own as an ending to the extract. Make sure it is in a style that fits the rest of the writing. *(2 marks)*

Ken and the potato

1 It was the potato that did it – not Ken. It was just too big and slippery for him. Well, that's what he tells anybody who asks him about it. But not many boys dare do that.

Ken and the boys were playing around in Park Road last Saturday evening. It was getting dark when Paul found a small pile of potatoes at the side of the road.

5 "Hey! Look! Spuds – oodles of 'em!" he told the gang. "Must of come off a van."

To show that he was happy to share the potatoes, Paul picked one up and hurled it at Eddie. That was the start of a short but hectic battle, with potatoes sailing to and fro until one hit Ken in the back. Ken is not the sort of boy to take insults lightly. He wanted revenge. He groped around in the semi-darkness, found a large potato and sent

10 it on its way with more strength than skill.

CRASH! Pieces of a large window in Mrs Brown's parlour clattered onto the rock garden below.

The boys stood petrified by their crime. Mrs Brown could take them all on (including Ken) and wipe the floor with them. Then, in a panic, they raced off like scared rabbits. Ken and Paul ran past their homes without pausing, finally stopping 50

15 metres up the road for Ken to recover and analyse the situation.

"Come on," Ken said. "Let's go home. We were just out for a walk, right? Don't even know what a spud looks like, we don't, eh?"

Paul nodded. "Never seen one in me life," he agreed. "I ain't thrown nothing at

20 nobody."

The boys turned round and walked home. By the time he reached his front door, Ken had convinced himself that somebody else had thrown the potato.

Take up the challenge! ●

Read the extract above and then answer the questions about it. *(20 marks)*

1 Why does the author use a dash in the first sentence? *(2 marks)*

2 Find four examples of colloquial language. Why are they used? *(4 marks)*

3 Find two places where the writer changes from a past tense to a present tense. Why does he do this? *(3 marks)*

4 The potato went through the window of Mrs Brown's parlour. What is implied by choosing the noun "parlour" instead of, for example, "lounge" or "living room"? *(3 marks)*

5 Which word has the author written in capital letters? Why? *(3 marks)*

6 Find five examples of time connectives in the extract. *(5 marks)*

unit 17

Describing past events

🔑 Key idea

Recounts of past events often contain these features:
- chronological account of an event as it happened;
- description of place or context;
- a statement of the impact or consequences of the event;
- past tense verbs, both active and passive;
- time connectives.

Train derailment

In August 1894, a new railway line was built by British engineers in Malaya. A few weeks later, men arrived and erected a unique notice at the side of the track. This is the story behind the notice and what it said.

1   In September 1894, a train set off on a 16-mile journey on the new line. The railway ran across land that had once been jungle containing tigers, leopards, rhinos and elephants. However, the passengers had no reason to anticipate trouble on what was expected to be a routine journey and they chattered away happily.

5   When the train was about three miles from its destination, the driver was surprised to see a herd of elephants ahead of him. Some of them were not far from the track, but the driver presumed that the noise and sight of his train would drive them away.

Events proved him to be wrong. A large bull elephant turned and moved ominously towards the oncoming train. The driver tooted the whistle on the engine, but this
10   merely enraged the bull. The bull raised its trunk angrily and then charged straight at the train. The force of the impact knocked the engine and tender off the track, throwing the driver into some dense bushes. The weight of the train crushed the elephant's head. In an instant, it was dead.

Eventually, the three carriages slowed down and came to a halt safely. The
15   passengers poured off the train and stared in awe at the body of the dead elephant.

In the end, it took five days to hoist the engine back onto the track and repair it. The elephant was buried near the line and, shortly after, the notice, mentioned above, was put up. It said: *"There is buried here a wild elephant who, in defence of his herd, charged and derailed a train on the 17th day of September 1894"* The notice still stands at the site
20   where the elephant died.

Try it out!

Read "Train derailment" and then answer these questions. *(15 marks)*

1   Say in one sentence what past event "Train derailment" recounts and where the event took place. *(2 marks)*

2   List four time connectives the writer uses to sequence events. *(4 marks)*

3   Why did the writer say "a new railway line was built by British engineers" instead of "British engineers built a new railway line"? *(1 mark)*

4   Find four passive verbs used in the passage. *(4 marks)*

5   "Events proved him to be wrong." (line 8)

    a) What were the events?   b) Who was "him"?   c) How was "him" wrong?

    (3 marks)

6   Imagine that you are a journalist. Make up a headline for the account.

    (1 mark)

The driver of the train had to write an accident report very quickly. Unfortunately, he made ten mistakes in his report. Find the mistakes and correct them. (*10 marks*)

On 17 September, 1894, we left Tapah Road on time at 1050 hours. We are pulling three carriages with approximately 100 passengers all together.

While we were about 3 miles from Telok Anson, we saw a large group of elephants at the side of the track ahead of us. They did not appear to be bothered by the train nor had not yet detected it.

Soon we drew nearer to the elephants, a large bull begins to move slowly towards the track, so I blew my whistle to warn it to keep away. The elephant ignored the warning and started to charge. It hits the engine on the left-hand side, knocking it off the line. I were thrown out of the engine and landed in some bushes. The tender behind the engine was also derailed and part of the track was damage. The carriages slowed down and stopped safely. None of the passengers received injuries.
I walked to the station at Telok Anson and report the accident to the station master.

The first woman doctor

1   In the 1840s, a young American woman, Elizabeth Blackwell, wanted to become a
doctor. At the time, there were no women doctors in the United States or Europe. The
idea of a woman becoming a doctor was thought to be ridiculous – women could not
even vote. Elizabeth applied to several universities to study medicine. Each time, her
5   application was rejected, until 1847 when Elizabeth applied to a medical school in New
York. The professors were reluctant to make a decision, so they passed Elizabeth's
application to existing students, thinking they would certainly reject it. However, the
students decided unanimously to admit Elizabeth. The university had no alternative, so
Elizabeth was admitted.

10   When Elizabeth arrived, she was introduced to the other students at her first lecture.
Her serious manner affected them positively. They no longer behaved badly during
lectures; instead they listened quietly and attentively. Although a few students tried to
distract Elizabeth, she politely ignored them and concentrated on her studies.
     In 1849, Elizabeth graduated at the top of her class – as the first woman doctor.

Keep practising! ●

Read "The first woman doctor" and then answer the questions about it. *(20 marks)*

1   The writer establishes both the time and place of the event she is recounting
in the first sentence. What are they? *(2 marks)*

2   Why was Elizabeth's application rejected at first? *(2 marks)*

3   In the first paragraph, where might be a good place to start a new paragraph?
Why? *(3 marks)*

4   What part of speech is each word below as it is used in the passage? *(4 marks)*
    a) women (line 2)   b) ridiculous (line 3)
    c) several (line 4)   d) unanimously (line 8)

5   Find three passive verbs in the passage. *(3 marks)*

6   Find four adverbs in the second paragraph. *(4 marks)*

7   List two examples of time connectives in the
passage. *(2 marks)*

How a single tear saved the lives of millions

1   The story started in the 1920s when Dr Alexander Fleming, a research scientist, was
     working in a London hospital. He knew that harmful bacteria entered a person's body
     through an open wound. The germs then spread, often leading to death of the patient.
     Dr Fleming wanted to find a way of killing the germs without harming the patient

5   His first step was to grow harmful bacteria in glass dishes. Then he tried to find
     something that could kill the germs. One day something brought tears to his eyes. A
     tear fell into a dish in which harmful bacteria were growing. A few days later, Fleming
     noticed that there were no bacteria growing where the tear had fallen. This showed
     him that it **was** possible to kill disease-bearing bacteria. He was more determined than
10   ever to find an antibiotic (or germ-killing) substance.

         Later on, he noticed a mould growing in one of his dishes near an open window. A
     microbe had floated through the window and had landed on the dish. All the harmful
     bacteria had died in a circle round the mould. He investigated the mould and
     discovered that it could kill many harmful bacteria. He named it 'penicillin'.

         Penicillin saved thousands of lives during World War II, and continues to do so.

Take up the challenge! ● ● ● ● ● ● ● ● ● ● ● ● ● ● ● ● ● ● ●

Read "How a single tear saved the lives of millions" and then answer the
questions about it. *(15 marks)*

1   The writer establishes who, when and where in the first sentence. What are
     they? *(3 marks)*

2   What part of speech is "London" in the second line? *(1 mark)*

3   In the first paragraph, what synonym is used for "bacteria"? *(1 mark)*

4   How does the writer link the first and second paragraphs? *(2 marks)*

5   Find two adjectival clauses in the second paragraph. *(2 marks)*

6   Why is "**was**" in bold type in the second paragraph? *(2 marks)*

7   What important quality did the tear and mould both have? *(2 marks)*

8   How do antibiotics help people to live longer? *(2 marks)*

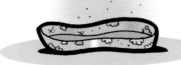

Giving instructions

🗝 Key idea

Instructions, directions and descriptions of procedures often contain these features:

- a clear statement of purpose;
- things (nouns) to use;
- steps showing the order in which to do things;
- imperative verbs;
- sequencing/ordering connectives;
- lists, numbers, letters, bullet points to signal order.

How to get rid of mice in your bedroom

You will need: mice, a humane mousetrap, cheese or meat for bait, sign saying "DO NOT ENTER: mice-catching in progress".

What to do

1 First, make sure there are mice in your room! _____ for black droppings.

2 Then, if there are mice, _____ the trap to make sure it is working properly.

3 Next, _____ a small piece of cheese or meat inside the trap.

4 _____ the trap near where the mice (or their droppings) have been _____.
HELPFUL HINT: Mice keep close to walls.

5 Then, close your bedroom door and hang the _____ on the outside to warn other people to keep out.

6 Inspect the trap once or twice daily. If necessary, replace any _____ that has gone.

7 When you find a mouse inside the trap, take the _____ outside and release the mouse some distance away from your _____, preferably into a field or wood.

8 Finally, repeat the _____ until there are no more signs of mice.

Read "How to get rid of mice in your bedroom" and then answer the questions. *(12 marks)*

1   Write five suitable verbs for the spaces in steps 1–4 *(25 marks)*

2   Write five suitable nouns for the spaces in steps 5–8 *(25 marks)*

3   What does the word "humane" mean? *(1 mark)*

4   Put the items in "You will need" in another format to make them easier to read at a glance. *(2 marks)*

5   Find four different sequencing connectives in the instructions. *(2 marks)*

6   Write another step that could fit between steps 6 and 7 *(2 marks)*

- Turn on your computer.
- Select "New message".
- Open your email software program.
- Type the email address of the recipient in the space labelled "To".
- Type the main idea of your email in the space labelled "Subject".
- Type your message in the main text area.
- Proofread your message and make any necessary changes.

Read the instructions above and then answer these questions. *(8 marks)*

7   What are these instructions for? Write a heading. *(2 marks)*

8   Which two steps are in the wrong order? *(2 marks)*

9   What could you do to make the order of the sequence clearer? *(2 marks)*

10   Write another step to go at the end of these instructions. *(2 marks)*

Mrs Clarke called in a plumber to repair a leaking tap. She watched him and wrote these instructions so that, in the future, she could repair a tap herself and save money.

1. You have to have a wrench and several different washers.
2   Find the mains tap and turn it off. It is often under the sink.
3   Turn on the tap and let all the water run out.
4   Unscrew the tap without damaging the pipe leading to it.
5   Take out the washer and inspect it. You will probably find that it is worn.
6   Put on a new washer.
7   Screw the tap on again.
8   Turn on the mains tap.
9   Turn on the tap you have just repaired. Check that the pressure is adequate. Adjust the mains tap if necessary.
10 Check that water is now flowing properly.
11 If the tap still leaks, repeat 2–9 with a different washer.
12 In the unlikely event that the tap continues to leak, call a plumber!

Keep practising! •

Read Mrs Clarke's instructions above and then answer these questions. *(20 marks)*

1   Why did Mrs Clarke write these instructions? *(2 marks)*

2   Write a heading saying what the instructions are for. *(2 marks)*

3   Which step is unnecessary because the same point has been made already? *(2 marks)*

4   Rewrite step 1 so that it begins with an imperative verb. *(2 marks)*

5   Combine steps 6, 7 and 8 to make a single sentence. *(2 marks)*

6   Which two steps contain a conditional sentence? Say what the connectives are. *(4 marks)*

7   Rewrite each of steps 2, 3 and 4 using a different sequencing connective in each. *(6 marks)*

Salmon and cucumber sandwiches

Wash your hands thoroughly. Fresh bread should be used if possible. If the bread is stale, you can pop the slices in the microwave for 20 seconds or more. That will make them softer. Two slices of bread per person. Open a tin of red salmon and tip it into a bowl. Don't drain off the liquid because it's good for you. Use a fork to mix the salmon in the bowl with vinegar and pepper. Spread the butter on the bread. The cucumber should be washed. Cut slices of it (with or without the skin – you can choose). Put the cucumber on the bread. Sprinkle it with vinegar. The salmon goes on the cucumber. Close the sandwiches. Cut them into quarters. Then eat them. A few slivers of cheese would go well with the sandwiches. Don't forget to clean up after yourself.

Take up the challenge!

(20 marks)

The instructions above for making salmon and cucumber sandwiches are difficult to follow, aren't they? Rewrite them, formatting them so they are clear and easy to follow. Remember to do the following:

- State clearly what the instructions are for.
- List the things you need – the ingredients and the utensils.
- Write out what needs to be done in correctly sequenced and numbered steps.
- Use imperative verbs.
- Use sequencing connectives to help make the procedure as clear as possible.

Extra challenge

Write your own instructions for how to write instructions!

unit 19

Writing reports

 Key idea

Report texts present information on a subject. They describe things as they are. They often include some or all of these features:

- verbs in the present tense;
- impersonal style;
- descriptive adjectives and adverbs;
- precise language such as facts and figures;
- arranged in an order of some kind – not necessarily chronological;
- headings and subheadings.

1 **The birds in my garden**

Every day I put nuts out for the birds, so many different varieties visit my garden.

Small birds

The smallest visitor is the tiny wren. It is only about 10 cm and hops between plants as
5 it searches for caterpillars and insects. The next smallest are various kinds of tits: blue tits, long-tailed tits and several others. Every morning these nervous birds dart down to eat the nuts and then rush back to the shelter of a bush or tree. The perky robins are territorial, bold and quick-tempered. They attack other birds, especially other robins!

Big birds

10 The bigger birds include blackbirds, multi-coloured jays and arrogant, strutting magpies who act as if they own the garden – until a passing crow sends them packing. We chase magpies away because they tear down the nests of smaller birds and eat their eggs and baby birds.

From time to time, larger predators can be seen.
15 Sparrowhawks (up to 40 cm in length) are sly but deadly. They swoop down, pounce on an unsuspecting bird and fly off triumphantly. Two-foot high buzzards use different techniques. They glide deceptively above the trees, calling out, "Mee! Mee!"
20 to scare smaller birds out into the open.

Read "The birds in my garden" on the page opposite. It is a report written by Adam, aged 11 Then answer these questions about it. *(20 marks)*

1   What is the purpose of the first sentence? *(1 mark)*

2   In what order are the facts in this passage arranged? *(1 mark)*

3   Find six present-tense verbs that describe the actions of the birds. *(3 marks)*

4   Find eight adjectives that make the description more effective. *(4 marks)*

5   There is one sentence in the report that contains a passive verb. Write out the sentence. *(1 mark)*

6   Why is a colon used in line 5? *(1 mark)*

7   Is a colon needed after "include" in line 10? Give a reason for your answer. *(1 mark)*

8   What is the effect of using a dash in line 11? *(1 mark)*

9   In the fourth paragraph, which of these words is not an adverb: deadly, triumphantly, deceptively? *(1 mark)*

10 At the end of the second paragraph, which word shows why robins attack other robins? *(1 mark)*

11 Where would be a good place to put another subheading in the report? Write the subheading. *(1 mark)*

12 Here are some other facts about Adam's garden and the birds in it. For each one, say where would be an appropriate place to include the information in Adam's report. *(4 marks)*
   a) According to legend, magpies steal any bright jewellery left lying about.
   b) Adam's house is in a rural area.
   c) Blackbirds are about 24–25 cm in length.
   d) Buzzards attack rabbits munching the grass.
   e) Robins scare other birds away.
   f) The birds like peanuts.
   g) The chaffinch is another type of small bird that visits the garden.
   h) Wrens are a brownish red in colour.

My brother

1 Bill is my brother. He is 14, three years older then I am. I do not remember him as a baby, To me he has always been very big – upwards, sideways and from front to back. He eat two or three times as much as anybody else in our family. In fact, he is like a mobile rubbish-bin, there is never any food left at meal times when Bill is there, so we call him

5 'V. C.' – the vaccuum cleaner.

I am not completly sure where Bill really lives. Mum lets him eat and sleep at our house, which is very kind of her, at other times Bill goes off to play football or rugby or whatever game is available. He has a black belt in marshal arts and a flat nose from boxing.

10 Bill has his good and bad points. He is very poplar at school, which is a good thing because nobody ever try to bully me now. Two big boys tried once, but Bill saw them. He smiled nicely at them and then held there hands (higher and higher up behind their backs) while he gave them some helpful advice. I have never had any truble since then. On the other hand, he has never been much good when he helps me with my maths

15 homework, I usually get poor marks because most of Bill's answers are wrong.

Keep practising ●

The children in Alice's class were asked to write about somebody they knew well. "My brother" is Alice's first draft. Read it and answer the questions. *(20 marks)*

1 How old is Alice? How do you know? *(2 marks)*

2 Find and correct six spelling mistakes. *(3 marks)*

3 Find four places where a full stop is needed in place of a comma. *(2 marks)*

4 Find and correct two places where the verb does not agree with its subject. *(2 marks)*

5 What figure of speech is "like a mobile rubbish-bin"? Why is it used? *(2 marks)*

6 Why does Alice call her brother "V. C."? *(1 mark)*

7 Why does Alice use the past tense in the middle of the last paragraph? *(2 marks)*

8 What would you suggest to Alice to improve the structure and order of the points she makes in her report? *(6 marks)*

My room

1 We have three "real" bedrooms in our house, but mine is not one of them: one bedroom is for my parents, one for my older sisters and one for my grandmother. My room is on part of the upstairs landing. It is known in my family as "The Cage".

My father (who is a carpenter) built it himself. He blocked off the end of the
5 landing and put in bunk beds. I sleep on the top bunk. He took out the bottom bunk bed and installed a table there. I use that as a desk, and that is where I have my computer and TV. When it is time to go to bed, I climb up a short ladder and – hey presto! – I'm in bed.

When you enter my room, the workspace is on the right, with my bed high above
10 it. On the left, there is a tall floor-to-ceiling cupboard with sliding doors. Don't be tempted to open the doors! The cupboard is full of clothes and accumulated junk. At the far end of the room, there is a window, which overlooks the back garden.

Although it is small and very cramped, my room is warm and comfortable. There is a radiator behind the desk, so I never feel chilly. We cannot afford to move to a bigger
15 house, so I just have to settle for my space on the landing.

Take up the challenge! •

Mike had to write a report about "My room" at school. Read what he wrote and then answer the questions about it. *(20 marks)*

1 What is the purpose of the first paragraph? *(2 marks)*

2 What is unusual about Mike's bedroom? *(1 mark)*

3 Why is a colon used after "them" in the first sentence? *(1 mark)*

4 Mike has used an informal style in some places that is not appropriate to report texts. Find two examples and say what is inappropriate about them. *(4 marks)*

5 Think of a subheading for each paragraph that summarises the main idea of the paragraph. *(4 marks)*

6 In the last paragraph, find three main clauses and three subordinate clauses. *(6 marks)*

7 Why do you think Mike's bedroom is called "The Cage"? *(2 marks)*

Persuasive writing

🔑 Key idea

Persuasive writing aims to influence the reader towards a particular opinion. It often has some or all of these characteristics:

- powerful, often emotional words;
- figurative devices (such as alliteration);
- imperative verbs to urge action;
- present tense verbs to state facts;
- sequencing and reasoning connectives;
- use of presentational devices (capital letters, bold, italics).

A

FOR SALE

A leading manufacturer has just had a big export order cancelled because of the recession overseas. As a result, we are able to supply pairs of men's and women's bicycles at the really low price of £100 with free delivery. Sturdy frame, leather saddle, choice of colours.
Hold-fast pedals. Free name stickers.

B

BUY ONE SUPER BIKE, get one FREE!!!
Huge DISCOUNT

- ACE suspension • 16-speed gears
- 26" alloy wheels • Latest brakes
- £85 only – deluxe model
- Free 14-day trial
- 12 months guarantee

Delivered directly to your home

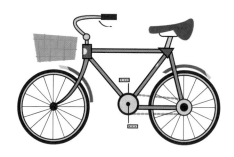

Compare the two advertisements for bicycles on the page opposite. Then answer these questions. *(20 marks)*

1   Which advertisement looks more attractive? Give three reasons for your answer. *(3 marks)*

2   a) Company B charges £15 for delivery. How do the total prices compare? *(1 mark)*

    b) Why does Company B not mention the delivery charge? *(1 mark)*

3   a) In advertisement A, find two words which may have a negative effect on readers. *(1 mark)*

    b) In advertisement B, find two words which will probably have a positive effect on readers. *(1 mark)*

4   Find the two imperative verbs. What are they? In which advertisement do they appear? *(2 marks)*

5   Both advertisements show only the top half of the full advertisements. What do you think is in the bottom half? *(2 marks)*

6   Company A is thinking of making the following changes to its advertisement. Consider each change. For each one say whether you think it will increase sales or not. *(5 marks)*

    a) Add: "Some assembly required."

    b) Omit from the beginning of the advertisement to the end of "As a result," and insert: BEST BIKE BARGAIN!!

    c) Change "really low" to "amazing" or "fantastic".

    d) Add: "Triple strength tyres".

    e) Change "leather saddle" to "plastic saddle".

7   From which company, A or B, would you buy a bike? Say which two things were the most persuasive in making your choice. *(4 marks)*

GREENACRES SCHOOL COUNCIL

Jumbo Jumble Sale Bargains!

Dear Parents

We are having a really **huge, magnificient Jumble Sale** from 3–6 p.m. on Saturday 10th July. There will be BARGAINS that you can EAT, WEAR, PLAY WITH and BOAST ABOUT to your friends! **Please** support us in one or all of these ways

1 <u>**BRING**</u> or send your jumble to school by 7 p.m. on Thursday 8th July. This is a wonderful oppertunity to clear out your cupboards. We will be most gratefull for anything – from your new Mercedes down to the remains of an old teddy bear. If you can't bring or send it, please phone the school secretry and we will arrange collection.

2 <u>**VOLUNTEER**</u> to run a stall or collect jumble. Even if it is only for an hour, **please** volunteer by sending your name through your child or by contacting the school secretary directly. NB: *Volunteers will be able to preview the jumble from 2–3 p.m.*

3 <u>**COME**</u> and buy. We need custamers. Therefore, we need YOU – people eager to snap up hundreds of bargains. So **please** come – and don't forget those fat wallets

All the procedes of the sale will be spent on improvements to the school – such as a better canteen, new sports equipment and books, and a fully equipped First Aid room.

Keep practising! •

The draft above is a letter (prepared by members of the School Council) which will be sent to parents. Read it and then answer the questions. *(20 marks)*

1 Find two examples in the letter of each of these features of persuasive writing:

a) powerful words and phrases; b) figurative devices; c) imperative verbs; d) reasoning connectives; e) presentational devices. *(5 marks)*

2 a) In what way might the heading appeal to parents? *(1 mark)*

b) Explain what effect the use of the word "Jumbo" has. *(1 mark)*

3 Find and correct six spelling mistakes in the draft letter. *(3 marks)*

4 Two punctuation marks are missing: at the end of the first paragraph, and at the end of point 3 Say what punctuation mark you would put in each case, and why. *(4 marks)*

5   What do you notice about how each of the three numbered points begins? What effect does this have? *(2 marks)*

6   What effect might the sentence in italics have on some parents? *(1 mark)*

7   Is this an effective piece of persuasive writing? Give reasons. *(3 marks)*

A

Mountain bike for sale. Cost £120 new. Recently repaired. Great value. Byer collects. Phone after 6 pm. 032-876

B

£30 ono. Milo Deluxe mountain bike. Superb condition. Lots of extras. Phone after 6 pm 032-876

C

FOR SALE: Mens' bike, incredibly reliable, well maintained. Suit teenager. Ideal for hill-climbing and ralleys. Phone 032-876 after 6 pm.

D

Bargain bike £30 No rust. lst class condition. Top quality tires. Very little use. Contact Dave on 032-876 any day after 6 p.m.

Take up the challenge! ·

David is selling his mountain bike through his local paper. The ad must be no more than 20 words. He has written four drafts. Read them and then answer the questions. *(20 marks)*

1   Which same two words could be omitted from **A** and **C** to give more space for description? Why? *(2 marks)*

2   Some of the ads have spelling mistakes. Find and correct them. *(2 marks)*

3   What vital piece of information is missing from **A**? *(1 mark)*

4   Give three examples of strong, persuasive language used by David. *(3 marks)*

5   What information in **A** might have a negative effect? Why? *(2 marks)*

6   **B** begins with the price. Is this a good idea or not? Give reasons. *(2 marks)*

7   What does "ono" mean in **B**? *(1mark)*

8   What serious (and amusing) mistake is there in **D**? How might this affect possible buyers? *(2 marks)*

9   Which of the four drafts is too long? How can it best be reduced to the limit of 20 words? *(2 marks)*

10   Use the information in all the ads and the best persuasive language from each, to write your own version in not more than 20 words. *(3 marks)*

Writing discussion texts

unit 21

🔑 Key idea

Discussion texts present all the various positions that are held about an issue or topic – for example, both sides of an argument. Discussion texts feature:

- balance – presentation of both (or all) sides fairly, honestly, politely and accurately;
- modal verbs – *should* vote, *can* argue, *must* agree, *might* indicate;
- adjectives that show judgement – *good, bad, right, wrong;*
- connectives that introduce different points of view – *yet, on the other hand, although.*

Mobile phones – good or bad?

1 According to a recent report, mobile phones may be a danger to the health of users, especially to children. They produce from 1000 to 10 000 times as much radiation as a mobile phone mast – or so the experts claim. Scientists are not yet certain weather the radiation and heat from a mobile phone are dangerous or not, but they suggest that
5 parents should think twice before giving a young child his or her own mobile phone. If there is a danger, it may not become noticable until years later. When it may be too late to undo the damage.

On the other hand, the advantages of mobile phone are well known, parents can keep in touch with their children and vice versa, so the phones are a valuable safety
10 precortion. Children can use the phones to send and receive text messages at almost any time of the day. In addition, they can use favourite songs as ring tones and play various games. So, as a means of communication and a sauce of entertainment, they are very useful. Already at least 80 percent of children aged 11–14 have a mobile phone. Manufacturers claim that fears of a health risk are either false or unproven.

15 Nevertheless, health experts now recommend that children should use a mobile for texts rather than calls. In that way they can reduce the risk of damage caused by exposer to radiation when making and recieving voice calls.

Read the draft of the discussion text "Mobile phones – good or bad?" on the page opposite and answer these questions about it. *(20 marks)*

1   Find at least two examples of each of these features in the passage:
a) modal verbs;
b) adjectives that show judgement;
c) connectives that indicate opposition. *(3 marks)*

2   In line 1, could we use "are" instead of "may be"?
What is the reason for your answer? *(2 marks)*

3   In line 5, could we use "must" instead of "should"?
What is the reason for your answer? *(2 marks)*

4   Find and correct six spelling mistakes in the passage. *(3 marks)*

5   Find and correct two mistakes in the punctuation – one in the first paragraph; the other in the second paragraph. *(2 marks)*

6   Choose the right words to complete this sentence:

The damage mentioned at the end of the first paragraph _____ *(has, may, was) be done* _____ *(by, at, to) children.* *(2 marks)*

7   What does "vice versa" mean in line 9? *(1 mark)*

8   In line 10, which of the following can best be added after "precortion"? *(1 mark)*

a) against theft   b) against radiation
c) against trouble   d) against children

9   In line 12, which of these does "they" refer to? *(1 mark)*

a) games   b) means   c) mobile phones   d) children

10   Out of 1000 children, how many do not have a mobile phone, according to the passage? *(1 mark)*

11   How may texting help to reduce exposure to radiation? *(2 marks)*

Miss Ellis asked her class: "Would it be a good idea to make cyclists pass a test and pay for an annual licence before allowing them to use public roads?" Here are two views:

1 **Sandra:** Yes, I think that would be fair. All road-users should pay to maintain roads and build new ones. At the moment, only motorists have to pay. Cyclists use the roads free of charge. Another reason is that a test would raise the standard of cycling and make cyclists more careful. However, I think the cost of
5 a licence should be only about 10 per cent of the licence fee paid by motorists. Cyclists do not take up any space on roads or do any harm to them.

Danny: I'm defenitely against a test and fee for cyclists. To start off with, it would be unfair because cyclists are often to poor to have a car or they prefer to cycle to stay healthy. Another reason is that no goverment will ever agree with
10 this because it will lose a lot of votes at an election, so there will never be such a law. That's fine with me because I cycle to school. Also, cyclists are not allowed to use motorways, so why should they pay for them?
   Besides, bikes don't produce harmful exaust fumes, so we should encourage cyclists instead of punishing them.

Keep practising! •

Answer these questions about the text above. *(20 marks)*

1 In line 1, what connecting word can we use after "fair" to join the first two sentences and make a single sentence? *(1 mark)*

2 In line 2, what punctuation mark could we use instead of the full stop after "pay"? *(2 marks)*

3 Why does Sandra use "However" in line 4? *(2 marks)*

4 According to Sandra's argument, if motorists pay £180, how much would a cyclist pay? *(2 marks)*

5 Is Sandra's last sentence accurate? Give a reason for your opinion. *(2 marks)*

6 What could Danny use in place of "To start off with" in line 7? *(1 mark)*

7 Find and correct four spelling mistakes in Danny's statement. *(4 marks)*

8 For what is Danny giving "another reason" in line 9? *(2 marks)*

9　In Danny's last sentence, what phrase can he use instead of "Besides"? *(1 mark)*

10　With which of the pupils do you agree? Give your reasons. *(3 marks)*

Take up the challenge! ●

In an argument, it is important to choose your words carefully in order to be fair, honest and accurate. Choose the right words carefully from the brackets to fill each space. *(20 marks)*

Exercise *(is, are, may, will)*

It _____ widely accepted that exercising _____ help to keep you fit. Exercise _____ even help to reduce stress. Walking and swimming _____ popular forms of exercise. You _____ usually feel the benefits of exercise immediately.

Television *(all, most, a few, none)*

_____ people watch television for at least an hour a day. _____ of those interviewed (except two) think there is too much sport on TV. "Soaps" are watched by _____ people, but _____ of those interviewed admitted to it! Only _____ people think children should not be allowed to watch any TV at all.

Cycling helmets *(always, often, seldom, never)*

Cycling accidents _____ happen, but they are _____ reported in the news. Too _____, in my opinion, you see cyclists without helmets on the road. Most people, like myself, think cyclists should _____ wear safety helmets. Some say helmets are uncomfortable and they would _____ wear one.

Traffic accidents *(however, in addition, on the contrary, in spite of)*

The person who is mainly or entirely to blame in a traffic accident is often a motorist. _____, this is not always the case because some accidents are caused by cyclists or by careless pedestrians. For example, _____ safe pedestrian crossing places all along the main road, some pedestrians will take their chances and cross the road whenever and wherever they please. _____, some cyclists think they own the road, and weave in and out of traffic _____ having special lanes designated for them. Cyclists and pedestrians are not blameless. _____, they are responsible for many accidents.

unit 22

Investigating English expressions

Key idea

Proverbs, slang or colloquial expressions and idioms all show how we can use the English language in imaginative ways to make our speech and writing more interesting.

Investigating proverbs

1 Too many cooks spoil the broth.
2 Out of sight, out of mind.
3 Wise men think alike.
4 Nothing ventured, nothing gained.
5 The early bird catches the worm.
6 Don't meet trouble half way.
7 Make hay while the sun shines.
8 Half a loaf is better than none.
9 First come, first served.
10 He who hesitates is lost.
11 Many hands make light work.
12 A bird in the hand is worth two in the bush.
13 Look before you leap.
14 Let sleeping dogs lie.
15 Fools seldom differ.
16 Absence makes the heart grow fonder.

Try it out!

Read the proverbs above. Do you know what they all mean? *(10 marks)*

1   Which proverb is opposite in meaning to (1)?

2   Which proverb is similar in meaning to (5)?

3   Which proverb is similar in meaning to (14)?

4   Which proverb is opposite in meaning to (16)?

5   Which three proverbs mean roughly "Make the most of your opportunities"?

6   Which two proverbs mean roughly, "Stay out of trouble!"?

7   Which proverb is somewhat similar and yet opposite to (3)?

8   Mr White hoped to sell his car for £1200 but, in the end, he received only £600 for it. When he grumbled to his wife about this, she answered with a proverb. Which one?

9   Mrs White and her daughter were putting up some shelving. Mr White offered to help them, but they did not want any help. Which proverb did they say to him?

10 Explain why "Let sleeping dogs lie" is sometimes good advice?

Keep practising! •

Match the underlined *idiom* in each sentence with its meaning below. *(8 marks – 0.5 mark for each correct answer)*

1   By agreeing to take on the project, they had <u>bitten off more than they could chew</u>.

2   Let's shake hands and <u>bury the hatchet</u>.

3   Miss Clarke <u>took a dim view</u> of Tom's excuses for not doing his homework.

4   In his descriptions of Victorian London, Dickens really <u>goes to town</u>.

5   What's wrong? You really look <u>down in the dumps today</u>.

6   Dad has started a building company and is looking for somebody <u>to do the donkey work</u>.

7   Hanya is so conceited. She's always <u>blowing her own trumpet</u>.

8   Help! I can't <u>make head nor tail</u> of those instructions.

9   If you don't <u>turn over a new leaf</u>, I'll <u>give you a piece of my mind</u>.

10 The surprise party was a bit of <u>washout</u> because someone had <u>spilled the beans</u>.

11 The working holiday was no <u>bed of roses</u>; everyone was expected to <u>pull their weight</u>.

12 The owner of that shop is beginning to <u>feel the pinch</u> and can't <u>make ends meet</u>.

a) boasting
b) change how you act or behave
c) disapproved of
d) do a fair share of the work
e) do the hard work
f) does it thoroughly
g) earn enough money to live on
h) easy or comfortable situation
i) experience financial hardship
j) failure
k) forgive and forget our differences
l) revealed secret information
m) taken on more than they could do
n) tell you truthfully what I think
o) understand
p) unhappy

13 Choose two of these idioms and write a sentence for each that shows you
    know the meaning. *(2 marks)*

    up a creek without a paddle   bang one's head against a brick wall
    keep one's head above water   hit the nail on the head

Take up the challenge! ●

**Rewrite each of these speech bubbles in standard English to show that you
understand the slang or colloquial expressions used.** *(10 marks)*

1 Cut that out. You're doing my head in!

2 What? Can't get my head round that.

3 Ugh! Doing homework is a real grind.

4 What a grotty-looking dump! And boy does it pong!

5 Sorry. Can't go. I'm skint.

6 Turn off the goggle-box and stop being such a couch potato.

7 Oh, she's just a pop-star wannabe, hoping to kick-start her career.

8 Don't hang around with them. They're really bad news.

9 Don't act so stroppy. Just play it cool.

10 Did you really fork out all that dosh for this clapped out car?

Extra challenge ●

Explain the difference between a proverb, an idiom and a slang or colloquial
expression.

Assessment 3

Using the right verb form

For each space, write a suitable form of the verb in brackets. *(6 marks – 0.5 mark for each correct answer)*

One day a popular TV host (1)_____ (hear) music (2)_____ (come) from the busy street outside his house. When he looked out, he (3)_____ (discover) a man, a dog and a horse. The dog (4) _____ (play) a guitar while the horse sang beautifully – and the man (5)_____ (collect) pennies in a hat from amazed people who (6)_____ (pass) by.

   The TV host (7)_____ (is) so impressed that he offered the man and his animals an extremely well-paid job on his TV programme. It was all agreed, but on the day they were due to start, the man and his animals failed to turn up at the TV studio. When the TV host (8)_____ (go) back home, he noticed the man and his animals in exactly the same place, playing in the street for passers-by.

   "Hey! What is the matter with you?" the TV host (9)_____ (ask) the man incredulously. "You (10)_____ (make) 100 times the amount of money you're collecting now if you appeared on my show!"

   "I know," said the man solemnly, "but it would have been a lie and I (11)_____ (deceive) the TV audience. The truth is that my horse cannot (12)_____ (sing). My dog is a ventriloquist."

Parts of speech

Answer these questions about the joke in the activity above. *(4 marks – 0.5 mark for each correct answer)*

1   Find an exclamation.
2   What part of speech is "lie" in the last paragraph?
3   What part of speech is "from" in the first paragraph?
4   What part of speech is "who" at the end of the first paragraph?
5   Find an adverb in the last paragraph.
6   Find the verbs in the last sentence of the first paragraph.
7   Find two adjectives in the first sentence.
8   What does the pronoun "they" refer to in the second paragraph?

Is it "a" or "an"?

Decide whether to put "*a*" or "*an*" in each blank space. *(5 marks – 0.5 mark for each correct answer)*

1 There is _____ historical monument in the centre of town.

2 This is _____ one-way street because it is very narrow.

3 The story takes place in _____ universe light years from our own.

4 Slow down! We're coming to _____ S-bend. It's _____ well-known accident spot.

5 Paul has just had _____ X-ray of his left arm. He broke it in _____ accident when he was playing football this morning.

6 There's a mistake in your first sentence. You've left _____ "n" out of that word.

7 Do you know of _____ European country that has _____ area called Brittany?

Using capital letters

Put in capital letters where needed. *(10 marks – 2 marks for each sentence with correct capital letters)*

1 It is well known that the temperature in the north of Scotland in january and february is lower than it is in London, but the temperature is higher in north Africa at that time of the year.

2 "When you've finished your english homework," mrs Baker said to Paul, "make sure that you put your books away and don't leave them on the table."

3 Cardiff is in south wales. It is about 50 kilometres west of bristol.

4 "The first monday in may is usually a holiday," my father told us, "so we can have a barbecue in the garden if the weather is fine."

5 In the novel *Great expectations*, by charles dickens, the action takes place during victorian times – that is, in the second half of the nineteenth century.

Joining sentences *(5 marks)*

Use the information in each group of expressions to make one sentence each time. Do not use "and" or "but". You can change, add or omit words. *(5 marks)*

1   Ruby liked the red dress. She decided not to buy it. It was too expensive.

2   You bought some apples yesterday. Where have you put them? You bought them at the farmers' market.

3   That's the house. My new friend lives there. She is from India.

4   The woman was very angry. Her car was damaged. The other motorist refused to pay for the damage. He claimed that it was not his fault.

5   My father worked in a factory. It has closed down. He has changed his job.

Prepositions

Put a suitable preposition in each blank space.

(10 marks – 0.5 mark for each correct answer)

Daft Dan (1)_____ London was looking (2)_____ a new car. So he went (3)_____ the street and (4)_____ a car showroom (5)_____ his house. Immediately, he spotted a red sports car (6)_____ a soft top that took his fancy. He walked (7)_____ the floor (8)_____ where the salesman was sitting.

    "Is that a really fast car?" he asked pointing (9)_____ the red car.

    "Fast!" exclaimed the salesman. "Why, if you got (10)_____ the wheel now and went off (11)_____ the motorway, you'd be in Aberdeen (12)_____ two o'clock in the morning. Do you want to buy it?"

    "Well, I'm not sure," replied Daft Dan. "Can I look (13)_____ the bonnet before I decide?"

    "Of course," said the salesman. "Take as long as you need."

    So Daft Dan lifted the bonnet (14)_____ the car and had a good look, but he still wasn't sure. So he decided to go home and think (15)_____ it

    The next day he went back to the car showroom. "I have decided I don't want to buy the car," he told the salesman.

    "Why not?" asked the salesman, (16)_____ just a hint (17)_____ disappointment (18)_____ his voice.

    "Because I stayed awake all night long," said Daft Dan, "and I couldn't think (19)_____ a single reason why I would want to be in Aberdeen at two o'clock (20)_____ the morning."

Say it another way

Rewrite these sentences, using the words in brackets and making any other changes that are necessary. *(5 marks – 0.5 mark for each correct answer)*

1   It is not necessary for you to wash the dishes. (need)

2   A hurricane blew down many trees last night. (blown)

3   The police will soon catch both of the robbers. (caught)

4   Mary was unwise to argue with Miss Evans about such a trivial point. (It)

5   The plumber explained to us the best way to repair the tap. (how)

6   The game should start now. (time)

7   I spent half an hour solving the problem. (It took)

8   The woman said that the man had tried to snatch her bag. (accused)

9   An explorer's life can be very exciting and dangerous. (full of)

10 How did the woman manage to open the door? (Mary wondered)

Reported (indirect) speech

Change these sentences into reported (indirect) speech. *(5 marks – 0.5 mark for each correct sentence)*

1   "I may come and see you tomorrow," Matthew told me on the phone.

2   "We'll wait for you at the station," the two girls told Ashra. "Try not to be late."

3   "Please can you tell me the way to the airport?" a tourist asked my brother.

4   My mother said to me, "Have you finished your homework yet?"

5   Davina said to me, "I'm going into town. Do you want to come with me?"

6   "Was anybody hurt in the fire?" I asked Daljit.

7   Paul asked his mother, "Have you seen my purple shirt?"

8   The stranger asked us, "Has the last bus gone already? Where's the nearest place I can get a taxi?"

9   Tony asked his sister, "Can I borrow your bike on Saturday? I'll return it on Sunday morning."

10 Tom asked Susan, "Do you still live in Trenton Road or have you moved to Stanton already?"

Punctuation

Rewrite the following passage, punctuating it so that it is easier to read and the meaning is clear. *(15 marks)*

We entered the ruins of the old house cautiously it was dark and gloomy inside. The windows which were boarded up kept the light and air out creating damp and musty air inside. We moved slowly along the corridor not knowing what to expect next. When we reached the first room the door was closed Be careful I warned we don't know what we might find inside.

Disregarding my warning Mike opened the door and ventured forth the rest of us crept loyally in behind him flashing our torches from side to side. Relief flooded over us there was nobody in the room and no obvious signs that the room had been inhabited recently.

We were just starting to relax a bit when we heard the sound a groan or maybe it was a sigh. It's coming from over there I whispered fearfully pointing to what looked like a pile of rags in the far corner. We approached the pile of rags nervously who or what might be hiding there

Uncertain what to do next Mike prodded the rags gingerly with his stick half expecting something large and wild to leap out of them again we heard the sound definitely a groan the hair on the back of my neck stuck out like the spines on a hedgehog. We all shone our torches on the rags and watched as Mike pulled some of them away then we gasped when the head and face if that's what we could call it of a tiny weird creature peered up at us dazzled by the light from our torches

Choose the word

Choose the right words from the brackets. *(10 marks – 1 mark for each correct answer)*

1   (Unless, If, Since) we had (go, going, gone, went) earlier, we wouldn't have missed the fireworks.

2   I won't be any good. (Its, It's) the first time I (play, am playing, have played) table tennis.

3   They continued walking (while, until, before) they (came, come) to a fork in the road.

4   Passengers (which, who, whom) are careless might leave (they, their, there, they're) bag on a bus.

5   Tom is late. (Maybe, May be) he has been delayed (by, buy, bye) the traffic.

Glossary

active and passive verbs

When a verb is **active**, the subject does the action to an object. The action moves from left to right:

The police arrested two robbers.

When a verb is **passive**, the person(s) who did the action follow the verb or are not mentioned at all because they are unknown or of less importance. The action moves from right to left:

Two robbers were arrested.
See also **voice**.

alliteration

Repetition of the same consonant sound in successive words. The repetition is usually at the beginning of each word: *a short sharp shock*.

articles

"The" is called the **definite** article because it refers to a known person or thing. "A" and "an" are called **indefinite** articles because they do not refer to a specific person or thing. We use "an" (instead of "a") if the next word starts with a vowel sound when it is spoken.

asterisk (*)

A punctuation mark put before a word to draw the reader's attention to information given about the word later on, especially in a footnote.

brackets ( ) or [ ]

Brackets are used to enclose information or an explanation that is additional and not essential because a sentence will still make sense without it.

comma (,)

A punctuation mark used to signal a brief pause. Uses of commas include:
- to separate items in a list:
  Some people collect stamps, postcards, foreign coins or other things.
- to mark off extra information or an explanation:
  Miss Wilson, the owner of the company, is a very successful designer.

- before and/or after the name of a person spoken to:
  Mary, have you got my scissors? Have you got my pencil, Luke?
- after a subordinate clause which starts a sentence:
  Whenever there is heavy rain, the stream near our house overflows.
- before and/or after direct speech:
  Peter said, "It's time for us to go." "I'm ready," Sami said.
- to mark off such words as "However", "as a matter of fact" and "indeed" when they are inserted in a sentence:
  My father grows lots of vegetables. However, he never grows flowers.
- to mark off a participle expression if it does **not** refer to the word immediately before it:
  The woman hid the blouse under her coat, not realising she was being watched.

complex sentence
A sentence made up of a main clause and one or more subordinate clauses:
The dog laughed because the cow jumped over the moon.

conjunction
A type of connective used to link words or expressions in a sentence:
We had to throw the fish <u>and</u> vegetables away <u>because</u> they had gone bad.

conditional sentence
A sentence containing a condition introduced by "if", "unless" or an expression such as "provided that" or on "condition that":
Plants soon die if you don't water them.
If you try to take a bone from a dog, it will probably bite you.
If motorists drove more carefully, there would be fewer accidents.

dash (–)
A punctuation mark that can be used in pairs to replace brackets, or singly to indicate a pause:
When we opened the box, we had a big surprise – there was nothing inside it!

infinitive
The base form of a verb. It usually has "to" in front of it: *to wish, to go, to be*

parenthesis

The term "in parenthesis" applies to a word or expression that is inserted in a sentence to explain or give additional information. Parentheses are brackets.
His hobby (if you really want to know) is collecting stamps.

participles

Most verbs have three kinds of participles: present (*eating*), past (*eaten*) and perfect (*having eaten*). The present and perfect participles can be passive: *being eaten, having been eaten.*

The present participle can also be used as a noun (*Swimming* is fun.) and an adjective (the *swimming* dolphin).

Simple Past tense

The main use of this tense is for completed past actions (*They were late.*), but it can also be used in these ways:

- in conditional clauses when we make a general statement or refer to an unlikely event:
  If motorists were more patient, they would have fewer accidents.
- after "I wish" and "if only":
  I wish I knew first aid. If only a doctor were here now!
- after "It's time" and "would rather":
  Hurry up! It's time you went to school. I would rather we went by bus.

Simple Present tense

The main use of this tense is for habitual or routine actions (*I walk to school*), but we can use it in these ways:

- in sports commentaries:
  Jackson takes the free kick. He passes to Jordan.
- for scheduled future actions:
  We leave next Saturday and return ten days later.
- in newspaper headlines even when they refer to past actions:
  MAN LOSES LEG IN SHARK ATTACK
- for future actions after "when", "if", "before", "after" and "until":
  Wait until Gran comes next Saturday.
  The flood will recede if/when the rain stops.

voice

A term used to indicate the relationship between the subject and the action. Voice can be *active* or *passive*. See also **active and passive verbs**.